BORDERS, BOMBS, AND...

TWO RIGHT SHOES

WWII through the Eyes of
a Ukrainian Child Refugee Survivor

Text illustrated with photographs, documents,
and historical data

LARISSA M. L. ZALESKA ONYSHKEVYCH

*On the cover: passport photo of the author in 1943,
after she was misidentified and arrested.*

ISBN: 0692746544
ISBN-13: 9780692746547

*Charleston, SC: Printed by CreateSpace, an Amazon.com
Company, 2016.*

To my Grandchildren

Lukash, Ruslan, and Roman Onyshkevych
Danylo and Sophia Leshchyshyn

CONTENTS

PART TWO: FACTS BEHIND AND BEYOND MY JOURNEY

Chapters

N.B. Ukrainian surnames, geographical names, and individuals words are transliterated in this book according to the Romanization Table for the Ukrainian Language, as provided by the U.S. Library of Congress and the American Library Association (1991). Exception: when the individuals are knownby differently spelled names.

"Memory... is the diary that we all carry about with us."
Oscar Wilde

PREFACE

Ah, that diary in our minds! Many of us have special projects dear to one's heart that we would like to achieve, to accomplish! These dreams, however, often become victims of our more pressing undertakings, and find themselves on a waiting list of our priorities. But the gleam of the idea, that spark in our own thoughts about writing a memoir, keeps burning until it takes over our consciousness. Then, one day, it suddenly shocks us with the announcement: "It's time!" It's time to transmit to paper that "diary" that exists in our thoughts. And, finally, we decide to actually do it.

However, a question may force itself: "But what was so distinctive in my life to deserve a memoir?" In my case, I claim that it was history. History and geography brutally affected the land of my birth, my distant ancestors, my family, and my childhood during WWII. Although my story includes many unconventional scenes and a multitude of trials and tribulations that had to be overcome, as so many co-travellers on my journey managed to do (though others did not), the fortunate individuals stand here also for the millions who faced similar experiences at other times, and under other totalitarian regimes.

My own memory has been filling up for years with minute details of my and my family's story; I have accumulated many varied and virtual files and folders filled with them. The decision to share these moments of the past isn't just for the sake of "did you know that?" – although, there may be some truth in this motivation, too. However, the bigger inducement is the realization that so many individuals, groups, and nations today continue to be suddenly ravaged and / or annihilated by historical events similar to those that I experienced. At times, one feels almost pressed to shout to the world "but did you not know, didn't you learn from history, or even from stories similar to what I, my family, and my compatriots had experienced only several decades ago?" This question has special relevance in the twenty-first century, when there is a new huge influx of refugees (including children!) seeking shelter in Western Europe, shelter from the destruction brought about by a new extreme ideology and its inhumane practices.

As a child in Ukraine, I experienced two of the worst totalitarian regimes that two invaders brought to my country: the Soviet and the Nazi. Then, still during WWII, I spent my preteens as a refugee in Slovakia, Austria, and Germany. The influx of refugees from Eastern European countries was driven by fear of what Russian communism brought to them only two years previously (while for most of Ukraine, it was for over two decades). Slovakia was our first stopover. The Slovak people readily provided aid to their fellow human beings, while keeping an eye on individual refugees, and registering our each move from town to town. The authorities needed to provide permits and keep track even when a group of 6 people went to the next town, to buy bread. In Austria, we experienced a typical Nazi transit camp structure, methods, and downgrading behavior towards us by those, who thought they were Übermenschen, and acted accordingly. After my family was released, thanks to a request from a German farmer needing us for work, we were on our own, trying to reach his farm. We were required to check-in with police at every stop along the way. The ever-present German need for order may be illustrated by the documents that I provide, where our each destination always depended on our next sponsor, who guaranteed our identity and presence. Even while the war was still on, and without computers, the regime was able to keep track of us all the time!

Then, immediately after the war, a new characteristic of many Germans surfaced: they were unwilling to share their meager, postwar food supply with the working refugees (most of whom were brought to Germany for slave labor) and wanted them to be repatriated immediately. In this respect, their wishes coincided with those of the Russians / Soviets (although, they had a different motivation and goal). People who have lost everything (from their family members to their country), and were stressed by the fear of the unknown, needed something stabilizing that would help them to overcome that insecurity. They needed a freely chosen purpose in their daily lives, and many found it temporarily in DP camps. The international organizations, UNRRA and IRO, fulfilled their humanitarian mandate to millions of refugees by sponsoring these camps. I purposefully delve into many details of the DP camps and their infrastructure, particularly as to how they managed to have a positive influence on the lives of youngsters and young adults there. Perhaps this experience of WWII refugees may bring some inspiration to those who work with the refugees of today.

It was World War II that brought incomparable losses, suffering, and havoc into the lives of individuals and their countries in Europe. In my memoir, many brief scenes of the reality that I had to face during the war, may demonstrate once again how some human species are capable of bringing utter devastation to others of our own kind. Still, at the same time, there are also examples proving that we can manage to survive even the greatest of adversities. Yet, in order to survive a life-threatening journey, it usually takes a helping hand from others, who thus prove their own humanity.

L.M.L.Z.O.

LIST OF MAPS

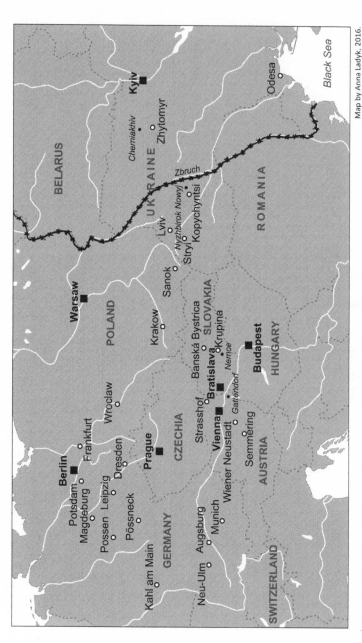

Map 1. My Family's Flight across Europe during WWII
Map by Ann Ladyk

Map by Anna Ladyk, 2016.

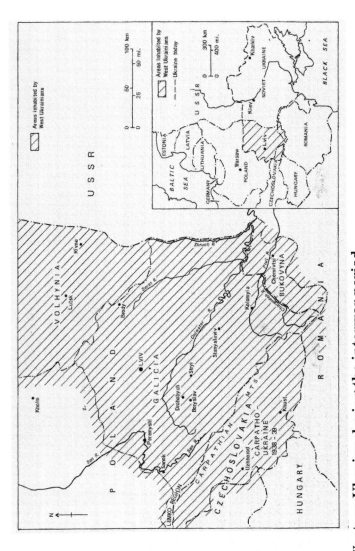

Map 2. Western Ukraine during the interwar period
Source: Published as Map 23, in Ukraine: A History, by Orest Subtelny, 1st edition, p.426.
©University of Toronto Press, 1988. Toronto, Buffalo, London. Reprinted with permission of the publisher.

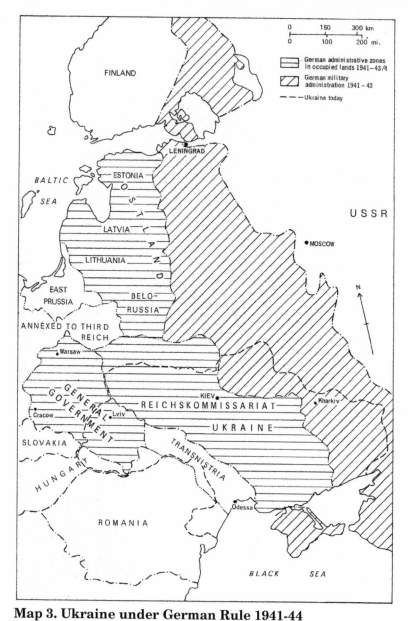

Map 3. Ukraine under German Rule 1941-44

Source: Published as Map 25, in *Ukraine: A History*, by Orest Subtelny,
1ˢᵗ edition, p. 466. © University of Toronto Press, 1988. Toronto, Buffalo,
London. Reprinted with permission of the publisher.

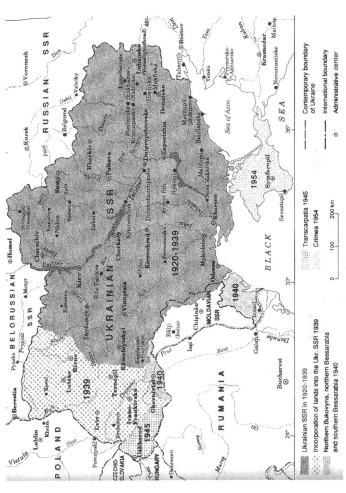

Map 4. Ukrainian Soviet Socialist Republic 1939-1945
Source: *Encyclopedia of Ukraine*, volume 5, p. 441. Edited by Danylo Husar Struk. © University of Toronto Press Incorporated, 1993. Toronto, Buffalo, London. Reprinted with permission of the publisher.

Map 5. Ukrainians in Displaced Persons Camps in West Germany and Austria, 1946-1950

Source: Published in the *Ukrainian Internet Encyclopedia*. Map drawn by Dr. Ihor Stebelsky. Reprinted with permission of the publisher.

PART ONE

MY JOURNEY THROUGH WWII

Chapter 1

A TRAIN RIDE, WOLVES,
AND A FUNERAL

It was the winter of 1941.
Yes, war was definitely underway.
Later, it was called World War II.

Mother received a telegram with the news that her father was gravely ill. She hurriedly packed our suitcases, and we took the train from Stryi (a town in the foothills of the Carpathian Mountains, in western Ukraine), going east towards Chortkiv and the Zbruch River.

I was six years old. I had travelled by train before, but only in daytime; I loved it. This time was very different. And, what a thrill it was: riding a train at night, my face pressed against the cold window, marveling at the sparks flying off the locomotive, which was powered by burning coal. Oh, and that unforgettable feeling of the unknown waiting just around the corner!

Travelling by night seemed like a unique opportunity to really get in touch with the train, with its promise of something exciting. I wanted a promise! The rhythm of the wheels always appeared to be confirming: *na-pev-no, na-pev-no, na-pev-no*! ["certainly" in Ukrainian, with a stressed middle syllable]. But what exactly where the wheels predicting "for certain"? Although it seemed,

3

Photo 1-1. My doll, Luba, and I

that occasionally there was a slight hesitation in the first syllable, which sounded almost like *ne-pev-no* ["not certain"].

We were on the way to the region where my mother grew up. She used to tell me some rather engrossing stories; like the one about the thousand-year old statue of Svitovyd that once stood several miles away from the village where Grandfather served as a priest. Mother said that it was only in 1848 that people found the Svitovyd statue near the Zbruch River. A few years later, some officials took it to a museum in Poland. That was about half a century before Mother was born; still, as a young girl, Mother and her siblings liked to go to that spot where the local people considered the now-absent statue not only a great local treasure, but also a symbolic protector that was taken away from them.

The word "Svitovyd" means in Ukrainian "the one, who sees the whole world." It is a four-sided statue, with a human figure depicted on each of them. While observing the world from all sides, at the same time, the statue may well reflect an emphasis and an awareness of events or threats that might come from any or all of the four sides. No wonder, that, in the middle tier, the four figures are holding hands, thus forming a symbolic closed circle, safeguarding each other, and also protecting the whole. The statue seems to depict constant vigilance in the face of a possible threatening external reality. After all, they do have each other's back, but at the same time the closed circle stresses an obligation to protect their clan, their unity, and/or their land.

But, that was all in the distant past. Now, standing far away in a foreign museum,

Photo 2-1. The ancient Svitovyd statue (now in a Krakow Museum) Courtesy of Vsevolod Onyshkevych

Svitovyd can't see and can't help its people, there, near the Zbruch River. But, perhaps, the distance from its native land is also its saving grace. Two world wars, several foreign armies recurrently marching through the land, could have destroyed the statue completely. However, the modern invasions and battles could have also served as a painful reproach to Svitovyd, that it didn't do a good job in protecting its own people.

I visited my maternal grandparents before. I remember Grandfather taking down from the top of an office cabinet a huge glass jar containing what we called "a head" of candy (it actually was the size of a human head!). With a special knife, he would chip off a piece of crystal-like candy, one chip at a time, and offer it to my cousin and me. And what a treat it was! Grandfather also showed me an unusual cross, on a long chain, which he wore occasionally on his chest. The darkened silver cross (about 3 inches long and half an inch wide) was hollow inside, and opened lengthwise. Inside, red plush lining cradled a chip of dark, dry wood: it was called an *encolpion cross*, believed to hold a tiny portion of Christ's True Cross. Grandfather visited the Pope in Rome on some occasion, and brought back that silver cross, which was believed to protect one from misfortune. However, riding on the train that night, I kept thinking more about the chips of the rock of candy, rather than the cross.

In the middle of the night, the train came to a halt at an uninhabited milk-train stop, rather than at a regular station; we chose it because it gave us a shortcut to the house. There, two men awaited us with a large sleigh, drawn by several horses, just like in a fairytale. The men helped us settle in, and covered us with heavy sheepskin wraps to keep us warm. What a wonderful and peaceful moment it was: I was all cuddled up in the fur, and so confident that nothing bad could happen to me!

Ilko Leshchyshyn, one of the men who came to meet us, quietly said to Mother, "The Reverend keeps asking whether you have arrived. He's anxiously waiting for both of you." Then he whispered something to her and we were off into the darkness of the night.

All around us were fields and fields covered with snow and ice. The sleigh made squeaking noises, sliding over the hard icy layer on top of the snow. Then, unexpectedly, in the opaque blackness in front of us, little gleaming orange dots appeared slowly, like mysterious summer fireflies. But this was not summer.

Ilko explained that these lights were the eyes of wolves, and that at night they appear to be distant little flickering fires. He stopped the horses and said not to worry, because he would drive the wolves away. I was in awe! We were left sitting in the sleigh, while he quickly built a fire that was soon throwing its own sparks in the direction of the wolves. As the fire grew larger, Ilko and his assistant walked around it, fanning it with blankets to keep the flame strong. It seemed as if they were performing some magic ritual dance. Gradually, the number of glowing eyes in the distance diminished, and finally all signs of the wolves' presence disappeared.

What a chilling adventure! And what a captivating night it was!

In a short while, we arrived at the village where Grandfather served as the parish priest. But this time, we weren't taken to the large rectory where we always stayed, only to a very modest and small hut, across from the church, nearer to the cemetery. There, in a tiny, narrow room, my Grandfather, or *Didunio Severyn*, lay on a bed. He could hardly lift his head. He beckoned for us to approach him, with his eyes focusing on me. He blessed me and kissed me on the forehead, and then blessed and kissed my mother. Several hours later, he was no more.

I could not understand why my grandparents were not allowed to stay in the large white rectory, with many rooms in the main section for the priest's family, and almost as many for the staff, and for the needy. For centuries, parish priests and their families had lived in such rectories. In the Eastern, or Greco-Catholic tradition, priests may marry before ordination. I heard it mentioned from time to time that Grandfather's line, the Shankovskys, had provided priests to this Ukrainian village and to the neighboring towns for four generations. The parishes belonged to Ukrainian Greco-Catholic Church, which is not Roman Catholic, but is Catholic and in communion with the Pope. Later, I came to understand what was happening: over a year before this, Russian-speaking Bolsheviks, or communists, occupied the country, and the regime was carrying out a plan to liquidate the Ukrainian Catholic Church and its priests. Only Russian Orthodoxy was to exist.

How did this happen? In 1939, Hitler and Stalin signed a joint pact of cooperation, and as a result, the Soviet Union took a large chunk of the western parts of Ukraine (which international powers had awarded to Poland in 1920, after the Ukrainian National Republic was overpowered by the Soviets). Thus the Soviet Union began to rule over most of Ukraine. My Grandfather was a victim of this new order – Russian-lead communism. What did these people want from him? At first, he was called every week to the NKVD (the Soviet secret police, precursor of the KGB) regional office, in the regional town of Husiatyn. There, they would question him about the reason why the parish was Ukrainian Greco-Catholic and not Russian Orthodox; why the Pope was called "His Holiness", and, whether this meant that Grandfather considered the Pope to be a saint? Being interrogated several times was a sign of worse things to come: arrest and sentencing to Siberia. Or – he could switch to the Russian Orthodox faith, or become an informer!

With the coming of the Russians/Soviets, the administration of the village was in the hands of the local Communist Council with two of their young activists, who were 19 or 20 years old. It was the custom of the Soviets to choose two local men to do the "dirty work," but each of them had to be from a different ethnic or religious group. Thus, one of the young men sent to throw my elderly grandparents out of the rectory was a Ukrainian, the other Jewish. The two young men physically threw my grandparents out onto a snow-covered street, and threatened with arrest any villager who would dare take them in. The Kravchuk family was one of the poorest in the village; actually, they were "the real proletarians," whom the communists claimed to represent, but for the moment were afraid to threaten. The Kravchuks dared to disobey the authorities and provide a roof over the heads of the elderly parish priest and his wife. After spending the first night out in the cold, Grandfather caught pneumonia, and this brought about his end within days. His death occurred because of these two communist activists, the two human "wolves," proved to be much worse than the real wolves we met riding through the icy fields.

On the night Grandfather was thrown out of the rectory, his *encolpion* cross vanished without a trace from his office. After he died, the communists seemed to have softened and allowed Aunt Stysia to take his body; they even permitted her to hold a viewing and a funeral service in the rectory. The body was placed on a high table (I could not understand why) called a *catafalque* (I couldn't understand that, either).

There was a discussion about the scarcity of flowers during winter, complicated by the fact that only chrysanthemums were acceptable for funerals.

Fate was not kind to the two young communist activists who forcibly evicted my grandparents. The Ukrainian man later had a life full of tragic mishaps. But even decades after the event, the locals did not wish to share the names of these young men. It was only 60 years later that, by chance, I learned the last name of the Ukrainian, but not that of the Jewish fellow, whom my Grandmother later selflessly hid from the Nazis. My cousin Dusia, who lived in the area for a couple of decades, would not tell me the name of the other young man. She said that there is no need to remember it or even hear it.

*Photo 3-1. Grandmother Lonhyna Shankovska and village elders,
who promised to protect her after her husband's death in 1941*

*Photo 4-1. In 1992, my cousin Dusia (or Lonhyna, on the right) and I,
at the grave of our great-great-aunt, with Mykola Kravchuk,
whose parents provided shelter to my grandparents*

9

Chapter 2

MY GRANDMOTHER'S CHOICES: FORGIVE THE WRONGDOER AND SHELTER HIM

Grandmother, or *Babunia Lonhyna*, was a singular lady, especially for her time. She had talents in the arts, speech writing, engineering, organizing projects, and most of all, helping people. Quite often, she was involved in planning and building large structures around the rectory. She enjoyed volunteering, planning dozens of community events and activities, such as reading clubs, theatre performances, and benefit balls. She used her writing talent to write eulogies that her husband would recite at funerals. It wasn't unusual for the family of the deceased to ask specifically that Grandmother write the eulogy, not only because it would be more obviously empathetic, but also because she was very close to all parishioners. And, besides the talents that she had, Grandmother was well known for always helping the needy, the homeless, and the abandoned.

Ukrainian Greco-Catholic (Eastern Church) priests may be married only before ordination, since taking the priesthood has to be their last religious vow. Thus, young men who completed their four years of basic theological study at around 22-24 years of age and wished to get married, were most likely to look for young ladies who would be between 17 and 24 years old.

*Photo 5-2. Babunia Lonhyna (nee Kalynovych) and
Grandfather/Didunio, Rev. Severyn Shankovsky (1889)*

In her late teens, *Babunia* married a future priest, and then
soon became the lady of a household with several servants and
more. This "more" represented anyone who was without a home
or without parents. She took them all in. Not only did she feed
them, she also clothed them – mainly in her own clothes. My
grandparents, *Babunia* and *Didunio*, had six children. When
most of them (the five who survived WWI) were settled in their
professions and working in various large cities, they would send
her the newest styles to wear. She looked so good in them! But
she never kept the new dresses and elegant shoes longer than a
couple of weeks, because there was always someone who was in
need of clothing. That is how all the needy women in the village
were often the first to be sporting the fashions of the day – the
dresses that *Babunia* received from her daughters, especially the
most fashionable ones from Warsaw and Lviv, where Aunt Sofia,
who loved the best and the newest styles, worked as a dentist.

At the time when *Babunia* got married, there was a significant
Ukrainian feminist movement. Women began to choose higher
education and professions. In 1887, the first Ukrainian anthology
of literary works and essays by women writers was well received
and shared by many readers, and so the idea of equal rights
for women was not something new to my grandmother. Like
her mother-in-law, who had acquired a profession only after

*Photo 6-2. Mother's sisters, Sofia and Stysia, strolling in Lviv,
before WWII*

she was married (she had four sons, was widowed at the age of
24, went to study music in Vienna, and then became a concert
pianist and music teacher), *Babunia* was determined to realize
her own dream of becoming an engineer. But in the nineteenth
century, women did not become engineers! So *Babunia* enrolled
in a correspondence college in Prague. Every week, she would
receive her lecture texts and assignments in the mail, addressed
to "Lonhyn Shankovsky." By omitting the final "a" in her first and
last names (Lonhyna Shankovska), which would have indicated
a female, she did not raise any eyebrows at the college, nor at the
post office, since her youngest son had that very name without
the "a" at the end. No one suspected that Grandmother was the
recipient of those thick foreign envelopes. Within a few years
after she started her studies, people were astonished to see new
structures popping up all around the rectory: a skating rink, pipes
delivering hot water to large bathtubs, experimental movable
stage sets and props for the village theater, as well as all kinds of
unexpected projects. She encouraged all her children to give her

a hand, especially in the theater: my mother was the artist and thus was in charge of sets, while Aunt Stysia was responsible for music, and my uncles were technical apprentices. It was only after Babunia died and the family found her engineering diploma that everyone understood where the know-how for all her new technical projects came from.

Grandmother's determination was apparent in all her choices, whether in helping an individual or a group, or dressing as she wished. A rather daring example of the latter was demonstrated when she attended a masked ball, in a neighboring town, to benefit the needy. While men chose such costumes as Zeus, Prometheus or the devil/Mephistopheles, *Babunia* (who always believed in equal rights for all!) decided to go as the chief she-devil. Although some of her friends warned her that it was not fitting for a priest's wife to appear in such an outfit, she designed it herself, and had it made by a dressmaker. The skirt had vertical flames shooting up as if in hell, and the design at the bosom featured flames coming

Photo 7-2. In 1936, at my grandparents' orchard: my grandparents, their three daughters with their respective husbands, a son, and three grandchildren (first row: I am standing and leaning on my brother; second row: Mother, Grandmother, Grandfather, Aunt Stysia with her daughter Dusia; third row: Father, Uncle Oles (Aunt Sofia's husband), Aunt Sofia, Uncle Lonhyn, and Uncle Ivan (Aunt Stysia's husband)

together as if under a boiling cauldron. It appears that everybody at the ball admired the outfit, and there were no whispers of any criticism in the family lore.

She demonstrated the same determination in more serious matters as well. In 1941, after two years of Soviet rule, came the Nazis, both of them uninvited. The majority of the population in western Ukraine was Ukrainian, a significant part was Polish, and there was a Jewish minority. The Nazis had daily quotas of Ukrainians or Poles to arrest or hold; those caught were

Photo 8-2. Babunia / Grandmother Lonhyna at a Benefit Costume Ball, 1890

either shipped to concentration camps or slave labor camps in Germany, or were shot or hanged in city squares as punishment for dissent or actions against the regime. Jews were rounded up extensively and were either arrested, sent to ghettos or to concentration camps, where most were summarily executed. The horrific Holocaust took 6 million Jewish lives.

After Grandfather died, *Babunia* went to live with her eldest son, Yakiv, who was known for helping Ukrainians and Jews who were pursued by the Nazis. He lived at the outskirts of town, near a forest. He turned his home into a transit stop for those needing to escape from the Nazis, just as two years later he helped Ukrainian insurgents who were fighting against the communists.

Naturally, *Babunia* Lonhyna helped her son in this undertaking. Uncle Yakiv knew what his mother was like, and warned her that his house was open to any victim needing help, except for the two young men who brought about his father's death. As fate would have it, one of these two, the young Jewish fellow, came to Grandmother begging to shelter him from the Nazis. Since she never refused help to those in need, the man knew well that she would not turn him away.

Then, two complications arose: the fact that she could not let her son know about it, and the fact that she had been ill for several weeks. While she hid the young man in the attic, it was only at night-time that she was able to take food up to him. To minimize the chance that someone might see or hear her, she lit her way with a candle (she could not use the flashlights popular at the time, since they were self-energized by hand-cranking, making a very loud noise, like frogs). One night, going up the ladder to the attic, with the food in one hand and a candle in the other, she tripped and ignited something along the way. To avoid discovery, she tried to fight the fire alone, while it spread quickly and soon threatened the roof. It was a cold winter night, she caught a bad chill, worsening her pneumonia, and died within a few days. The young Jewish man escaped.

I often wondered why the villagers kept silent about the names of the two young men who caused my grandparents' deaths. Later, I understood that identifying the men by their names was not considered the right thing to do.

And if the Svitovyd statue had been left in place nearby, would it have ignored the names of those two men as well? What else would it have seen and kept secret? Would it have judged all those who trespassed on this land, from the East and from the West, brutalizing its people?

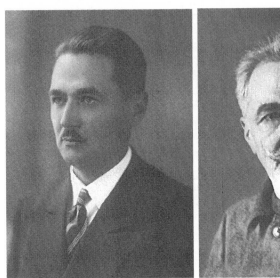

Photo 9-2. Uncle Yakiv in 1942 and 1955 (at the age of 58), after spending 10 years in a Soviet Gulag concentration camp

Photo 10-2. My grandparents' grave and headstone, showing the dates of their respective deaths during the Soviet (1941) and Nazi (1942) regimes

Chapter 3

WHY WERE THE COMMUNISTS RUNNING AWAY?

For almost half a century, few people knew that on 23 August 1939, Stalin and Hitler signed a pact of cooperation, officially known as the Molotov-Ribbentrop Pact. One part of this pact (which was a secret protocol) was an agreement to divide Eastern Europe, specifically Poland, with western Ukraine going to the Soviets. On September 1, 1939, Germany invaded Poland, and WWII erupted.

Because of the Molotov-Ribbentrop Pact, Soviet communist forces (whom everybody called "the Bolsheviks" or "Russians") occupied western Ukraine. A Ukrainian insurgent movement arose in opposition to the actions by the Soviets. For two years, the Soviet regime created terror, performed executions, and sent tens of thousands to Siberia, where many of them died. In April 1941 alone, in western Ukraine there were 38 incidents against the communist occupation, so the Soviet secret police received orders to liquate western Ukrainian insurgents. David E. Murphy cites that on 23 May 1941, the Soviets had "detained and loaded on freight cars for their journey into exile 11,476 persons." (*What Stalin Knew. The Enigma of Barbarossa*. New Haven: Yale UP, 2005, p. 34.)

*Photo 11-3. Soviet and Nazi soldiers shaking hands in September 1939,
29 km from the city of Stryi; road-signs point towards Stryi and Drohobych
(By permission of the Drohobyczer Zeitung)*

The communists specifically tried to eliminate most Ukrainian leaders and activists in the political, cultural, and religious fields. It was an attempt to leave the nation without leaders and identity. The Russians permitted only their own religion, and enforced their own language, in order to mold a Soviet identity, while demanding an adherence to the communist ideology. Signs in the Russian language appeared on posters. Some of my friends, who were a little older than I, and attended grade 1 or 2 already, kept showing me their textbooks. I remember a photograph of a large face with a huge moustache and devouring eyes; the man was holding a little girl in his arms, and receiving flowers from schoolchildren. His name was Joseph Stalin, and the girl that he was holding was his daughter Svetlana. This picture was plastered all over many books and posters. The communists aimed their ever-present propaganda at the young, as early as possible. (*Who knew that in the 1970s, Svetlana would live in Princeton, N.J., about 6 miles away from me, and I would see her there?*) In late June 1941, when the Nazis were pushing the Soviets out, the latter panicked before retreating, and furiously tried to hide signs of their more recent atrocities.

20

One weekday, Mother and I stopped at our church to pray, as we often did when passing it. On our way out the church door, we could see Miss Olha Kravchyshyn (Miss K.) on the other side of the street. She was to be my grade school teacher in the fall, and I was glad to hear from older children that they loved her. However, there was a rumor amongst many of her first-grade students that she had the ability to read thoughts. I believed that to be so. And here was Miss K. in front of us, holding a large thermos in her hands. Mother whispered that obviously some good souls were happy to share their lunch with her. At the time, the River Stryi flooded many farms in the region, making food and produce very expensive and hard to get. Miss K. supported her elderly, bedridden father and obviously was glad to get a ready meal for him. I was sorry for her, and felt rather guilty for suspecting that she probably could not afford to pay for her food. I did not want to embarrass her, so I quickly tried very hard to bring other thoughts to my mind, in order to somehow cover up my concern for Miss K.'s food situation.

On another occasion, Mother and I were running some errands. Along the way, we met a friend of hers, who whispered something so terrible that it upset both of them. Mother then told me that she would have to make a stop at Miss K.'s place, where I was to wait for her. I stayed with Miss K. for more than half an hour, talked a bit, and then became restless. Her apartment was on the second floor, and I had a good view through the window. Looking at the strange-looking building across the street, suddenly I spotted Mother going into the courtyard nearby. Somehow I felt I had to join her *immediately*. But would Miss K. let me? Being able to read my thoughts, she would know that I had no such instructions from Mother. So, without waiting for permission to leave, I quickly blurted out to Miss K. that I could see my mother and just had to go to her *now*. I knew this was not proper behavior for a 6-year old, but I felt that I had to discover what mysterious circumstances made Mother leave me with Miss K.

I ran across the street and passed through a gate in a brick wall surrounding that building. At first, I thought that it was part of some weird and dilapidated marketplace: there were heaps of clothing lying around the courtyard, and dozens of people were frantically running around inspecting something on the ground. When I got closer, I saw that people's faces were very intense and

21

many were crying. And there was such a horrible, penetrating stench! Many of the people were holding handkerchiefs over their noses. And it wasn't heaps of clothing lying around, they were human corpses recently covered with pieces of clothing. While I was trying to comprehend the situation, Mother caught sight of me, ran to me, and put her arm around my shoulders. She was shocked that I left her friend's apartment against her instructions. But there I was, so Mother quickly took me away from the courtyard. Only then, it dawned on me that the place was *a prison courtyard*!

That horrible stench was something I could never forget. It was the stench of charred human bodies, of open wounds, of decomposing flesh. Even more than seven decades later, to this day I can still remember that odor, and can always identify the smell of a long-standing inflamed wound. I am sure that the relatives and friends of those who were murdered there, who came to identify them, remember it also. Similar scenes took place in each western Ukrainian city and town on or about 22 June 1941, when the communists were retreating and tried to hide signs of their barbarity.

The large stone building that I was looking at from Miss K.'s window, located on the Third of May Street, was the city prison. The communists held hundreds of political prisoners there – anyone whom they in any way suspected of lacking blind submission to the Soviet regime, since such people could not be trusted and could turn against them. The regime held total power through terror tactics. Yet it took five decades to bring most of these horrible details to light.

On the night that the communists retreated from Stryi, they executed, burned or mutilated hundreds of prisoners, so that the corpses would be unrecognizable and there would be no trace of the victims whom they had held and tortured. In the prisons of each city in the western Ukrainian regions, about 24 thousand political prisoners were executed in such brutal manner.

*Photo 12-3. A logbook with documentation on prisoners
at Stryi Prison # 2, of the Drohobych Oblast / Region.
All records were in the Russian language. Photo by Oleh Piasetsky.
Reprinted with permission of Taissia Haidukevych, Ed. of Stryi, UkrPol 2007.*

*Photo 13-3. In the style of folk art, or art naïf, the picture below
depicts the essence of what I saw: people looking for their loved ones
or friends, and identifying the corpses. However, I remember several
rows of corpses, while the artistic rendering above shows only one row,
symbolically representing all of the 200 corpses found there. (Painting
by Petro Savchyn.) Reprinted with permission of Taissia Haidukevych,
Editor of Stryi UkrPol, 2007.*

Photo 14-3. This is the building that I saw from Ms K's apartment. After the fall of the USSR, the Stryi city administration turned the prison into a memorial museum, so that everyone could come to look at this place of sorrow, symbolized by the outstretched pointed fingers on the iron fence, and a Pieta sculpture in the courtyard on the right. The architect of the Memorial is Orest Skop and the sculptor Vasyl Yarych. (Photo by Oleh Piasetsky.) Reprinted with permission of Taissia Haidukevych.

As soon as walls of the Stryi prison were opened, documents were discovered with the communists' plans to arrest more "suspects or undesirable elements." To the communists, such terms meant community leaders and the "intelligentsia", that is, professionals such as teachers, lawyers, or anyone with a university education, people who studied or travelled abroad, as well as even some idealistic communists. Among the documents was a list of people to be arrested next. My father's name was on it. After all, he pursued graduate studies in Vienna, he was elected to Parliament in 1918, during the short-lived independent Western Ukrainian National Republic, he was a cultural community leader, an educator, and a Scouts counselor. For the Soviets, that was certainly enough to place his name on the list of "enemies of the people."

Chapter 4

ONE TYRANT FROM THE EAST AND
ONE FROM THE WEST
Or
WHO WAS THE CRUELEST OF THEM ALL?

Why do foreign countries invade their neighbors and start wars?
Is it always to grab more territory and more human and natural
resources? During the twentieth century, Russians invaded
western Ukraine on three occasions, though in two roles: the
first as a czarist army of occupation (1914), and then as Soviet
aggressors (1939 and 1945). The second time, they used the excuse
that it was because of the Molotov-Ribbentrop Non-Aggression
Pact (also known as the Stalin-Hitler deal of cooperation) of 1939.
They brought death and destruction to Ukrainians and Poles. And
the situation was repeated in 1945. A highly respected Ukrainian
composer and cultural leader, Stanislav Liudkevych, was forced
to "welcome" the Soviets from the stage of the Lviv Opera House.
The legend is that he proclaimed: "the Soviets have liberated us,
and there is nothing we can do about it."

In 1939, some left-leaning Ukrainians welcomed the Soviets,
since they hoped this would bring the end of previous Polish
mistreatment and administrative mismanagement discriminating
against Ukrainians (especially in higher education, in professions,
as well as in Scouting). Then, after the two years' experience under
Soviet rule, when the Nazis came in 1941, people believed that

things could not get any worse than during the Russian regime. The Soviets had just demonstrated their capacity for creating the lowest circle of hell, so how could anyone else be worse? After all, some of the German-speaking Austrian Kaisers (during the Austro-Hungarian Empire) had been rather benevolent rulers. Most Ukrainians (especially in the western part of the country) who had secondary and university education knew the German language. Many were forced to study in Vienna (since the Polish administration placed some limitations on Ukrainians pursuing university studies), as did those who had to serve in the Austrian army, or the Ukrainians who were elected representatives to the Parliament in Vienna. The cultures were quite similar. Thus there was hope that the educated Germans would behave like the Austrians, and would be more civilized than the uncouth and uneducated communists. The latter gave a bad name to all Russians and to their "proletarian" movement. However, the "cultured" Nazis, in their status as conquerors, besides playing "supermen," were also eager to take possession of material goods, art, and homes of the local population, and were not immune to the worst killings.

And then...

During the first couple of weeks of Nazi rule, Mother could still take me to a popular pastry shop in the center of town, near the train station.

Photo 15-4. The Stryi Train Station in the late 1920s

That cafe nearby served wonderful pastries and tortes, which I enjoyed there from time to time with a glass of milk. But then, probably in the fall of 1941, when we wanted to enter the cafe, there was a sign on the main door in several languages, proclaiming that the entrance was only for Germans. I remember that phrase well: "Nur für Deutsche"! It started showing up in so many places! At first it was hard for me to understand the concept of "For Germans only," but soon it became pretty clear, since it started affecting even a child's life.

The German occupational forces issued their own passports to us. In these documents, the country was not named, only that it was part of "General Government" (or "G.G." for "General Gouvernement")! For the description of "region" or "district", only "Galicia" [Halychyna] was used. While during the Soviet regime, passports were printed only in Russian, now, German passports were in the German, Ukrainian, and Polish languages. The Nazis identified a person's nationality, just like the Soviets did. On the passport cover, in large, bold letters were: U for Ukrainians, P for Poles, and J for Jews (Jews also had to wear a yellow armband with the Star of David).

Nazi documents, such as passports, school reports, or certificates, always included information about a student's nationality as well as religion (as may be seen on my certificate, below). At that time, there were three main religions in our city: Roman Catholics (mostly Poles and some Ukrainians), Greco-Catholic Ukrainians, and Jews.

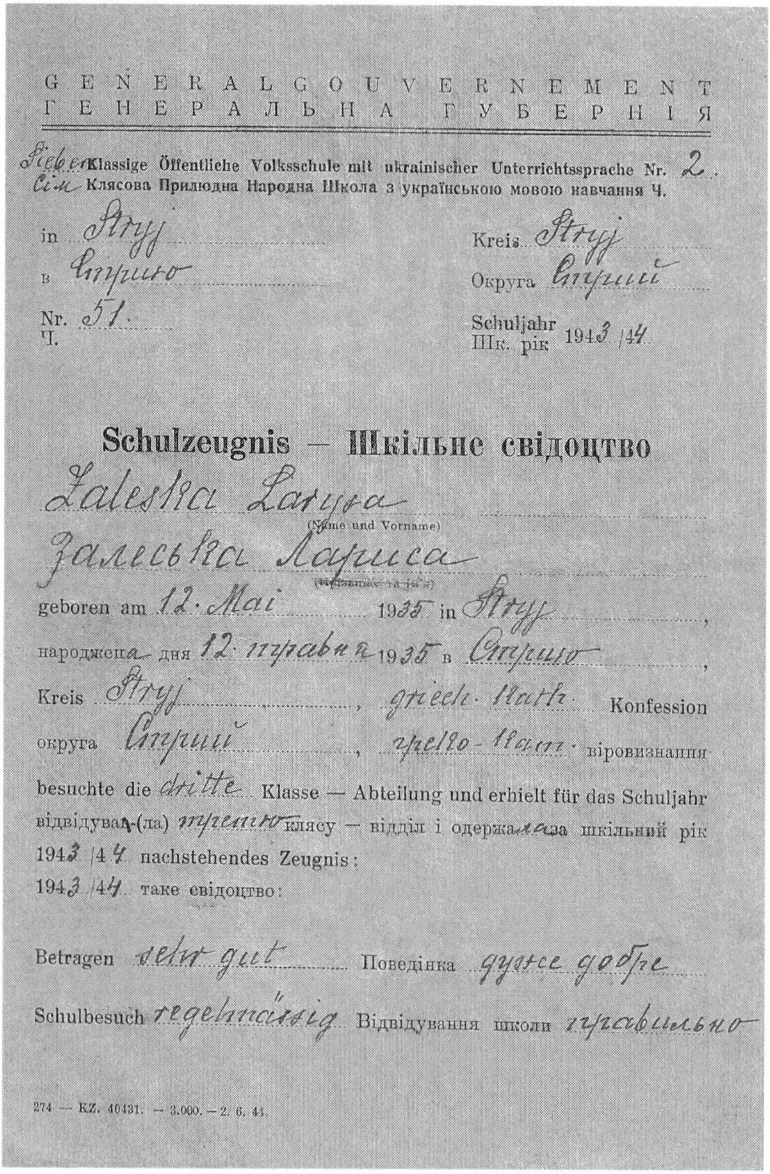

G E N E R A L G O U V E R N E M E N T
Г Е Н Е Р А Л Ь Н А   Г У Б Е Р Н І Я

*Sieben*Klassige Öffentliche Volksschule mit ukrainischer Unterrichtssprache Nr. *2*.
Сім-Клясова Прилюдна Народна Школа з українською мовою навчання Ч.

in *Stryj*   Kreis *Stryj*
в *Стрию*   Округа *Стрии*

Nr. *51*.   Schuljahr
Ч.   Шк. рік 194*3* /*44*

Schulzeugnis — Шкільне свідоцтво

Zaleska Larysa
(Name und Vorname)

Залеська Лариса
(прізвище та ім'я)

geboren am *12. Mai* 193*5* in *Stryj*,

народжена дня *12. травня* 193*5* в *Стрию*,

Kreis *Stryj*, *griech. kath.* Konfession

округа *Стрии*, *грецко-кат.* віровизнання

besuchte die *dritte* Klasse — Abteilung und erhielt für das Schuljahr

відвідував-(ла) *третю* клясу — відділ і одержа*ла* за шкільний рік

194*3* /*44* nachstehendes Zeugnis:

194*3* /*44* таке свідоцтво:

Betragen *sehr gut* Поведінка *дуже добре*

Schulbesuch *regelmässig* Відвідування школи *правильно*

274 — KZ. 40431. — 3.000. — 2. 6. 44.

Photo 16-4. My Grade 3 Report Card

28

Photo 17-4. An identification card for Ukrainians, issued by the Nazi regime on the cover of the ID card, the U stood for "Ukrainian." The text was in German (top line, in bold), Ukrainian, and Polish (in parenthesis). However, the Ukrainian text did not use the Ukrainian spelling of the time, only the Soviet spelling, substituting the Ukrainian "G" with an "H" for General Government. This indicates that the local Nazi administrative office probably included Soviet or Soviet-trained officials who wrote the text for the Nazis to use.

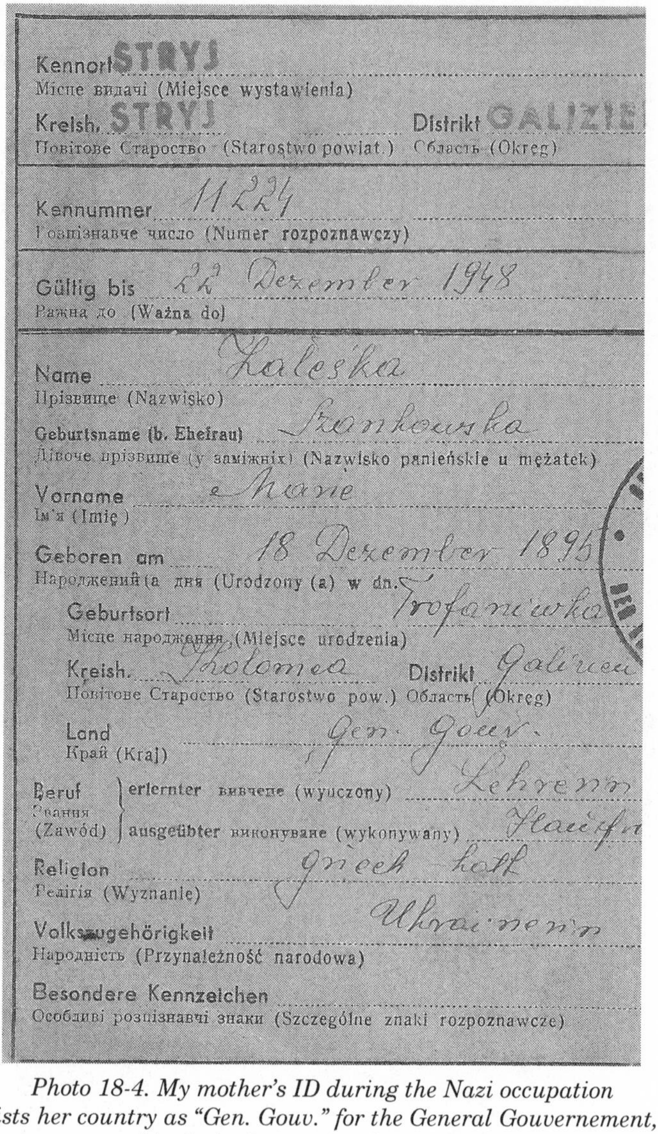

Kennort **STRYJ**
Місце видачі (Miejsce wystawienia)

Kreish. **STRYJ**   Distrikt **GALIZIE**
Повітове Староство (Starostwo powiat.)   Область (Okręg)

Kennummer *11224*
Розпізнавче число (Numer rozpoznawczy)

Güitig bis *22 Dezember 1948*
Ражна до (Ważna do)

Name *Zaleska*
Прізвище (Nazwisko)

Geburtsname (b. Ehefrau) *Szankowska*
Дівоче прізвище (у заміжніх) (Nazwisko panieńskie u mężatek)

Vorname *Marie*
Ім'я (Imię)

Geboren am *18 Dezember 1895*
Народжений(а) дня (Urodzony (a) w dn.)

Geburtsort *Trofaniówka*
Місце народження (Miejsce urodzenia)

Kreish. *Kolomea*   Distrikt *Galizien*
Повітове Староство (Starostwo pow.) Область (Okręg)

Land *Gen. Gouv.*
Край (Kraj)

Beruf ⎱ erlernter вивчене (wyuczony) *Lehrerin*
(Zawód) ⎰ ausgeübter виконуване (wykonywany) *Hausfrau*
Звання

Religion *griech. kath.*
Релігія (Wyznanie)

Volkszugehörigkeit *Ukrainerin*
Народність (Przynależność narodowa)

Besondere Kennzeichen
Особливі розпізнавчі знаки (Szczególne znaki rozpoznawcze)

*Photo 18-4. My mother's ID during the Nazi occupation
lists her country as "Gen. Gouv." for the General Gouvernement,
and includes her nationality and religion*

During the early months of the Nazi occupation, we rented a house with large glass doors opening unto a terrace. There was a large front yard shaded by beautiful trees. Mother loved to do her early morning walks and exercises there, followed by collecting fresh dew from the leaves of plants and grass, which she used as natural cosmetic moisturizers. But Mother's morning ritual did not last long. One morning they requisitioned the house, and that very evening we had to vacate it, including moving our piano. It was my great-grandmother's upright piano; Aunt Stysia had taken the grand piano, while Mother took the upright with two candleholders attached, to see the sheet music. (Mother felt very fortunate now that she was given the smaller instrument.) The Germans obviously couldn't be bothered with our pre-electricity upright, since they had requisitioned a nice grand piano from someone else.

Father had been a high school teacher for many years, as well as the director of The Stryi Ukrainian Teachers College for Women, so most of the town knew him. An urgent appeal went out among all his friends to quickly find an apartment for us. Miraculously, one was found (in a building owned by a colleague, Prof. Dubytsky), and about fifteen current and former students helped move our belongings, including Father's extensive library. This was accomplished mostly by carrying items in whatever box or suitcase was at hand; the only small truck that was available at such short notice transported our furniture. We must have made quite a procession, marching from street to street, all the way to the other side of town. I remember that we had to stop many times. Being about 6 or 7 years old, at one of stops I took the opportunity to show my schoolmates some of my cherished items, including golden chains with crosses, and Virgin Mary golden medals (these were the standard gifts that my Godparents gave me on my christening). For helping us out in our hour of need, I gave away some of these items as keepsakes to my friends. Obviously, Mother did not hear about this until many years later.

Photo 19-4. My parents and my brother at our upright piano

Our new apartment was on Lelewel Street, with houses built only on one side, facing a large park. Just behind it ran the Stryi

River. In front of the building were dozens and dozens of lovely white narcissi/daffodils, with thin red crowns surrounded by flat, white petals. I remember that very pleasant and distinguished narcissi scent even today. These flowers seemed to stand there proud and pure, in contrast to the events developing in the city, bringing various types of changes, including changes in street names. Each regime liked to *replace* street names honoring people associated with the previous regime, with names connected to the new one.

Photo 20-4. The house on Lelewel Street, as it looked in 1985, with new numbering; the street was renamed by the Soviets to Maria Zankovetska Street

During the Polish administration, our street was called Lelewel, in honor of Joachim Lelewel, a Pole who was one of the revolutionaries protesting the attempt by Russian Czar Nicholas I to make Poland part of Russia (1830-31). The Germans renamed the street Uferstrasse (Shore Street). Later, the Soviets allowed the street to be named in honor of a great Ukrainian actress, Maria Zankovetska (1860-1934).

After we moved to our new residence, at first we enjoyed the view from our street, facing the park and the river.

But that feeling did not last long.

One day, Father gave me two white angora baby rabbits. I loved to go to the park and pick cloverleaf for them. Sometimes I even took them "for a walk" to the park. On a particular day when I was there with my rabbits, Nazi policemen chased me away. A German officer who was posted in the building next door had noticed my trips to the park and saw the confrontation. He rescued my rabbits, brought them back to me, and told my mother that he did this for me because I reminded him of his own little girl at home. On another day, he gave me a pound of butter in a nice glass serving case (knowing quite well that butter was not available to non-Germans). But Mother told me to take it back to him, which I did immediately. I was not to accept gifts from the Nazis!

That park where I took my rabbits soon gained a very dark history.
One day, we saw trucks full of people being driven there.
Then we heard shot, after shot, after shot...
I soon learned that the Nazis were transporting Jews to the park.
But they never came out...

Immediately, the atmosphere in the town became tense.

People were afraid. When talking on the street, people would turn around to check who was near them and might be listening. I noticed that when people were talking to friends, they would often hold a hand over their own mouth.

During the war, people said that the main difference between the Nazis and the communists was that the Soviets arrested and executed people *in secret and at night,* while the Nazis did so *openly and in daylight.* While the Nazis would even use the terrorizing tactic of hanging people in the middle of city squares, the Soviets never admitted to any arrests or executions. The Nazis would even let it be known, ahead of time, the number of people that they were planning to arrest or shoot as *a reprisal,* and from which nationality the victims were to be taken that day. This was to create group pressure or group responsibility, discouraging any anti-Nazi acts: for one German killed or attacked, the number executed could be as many as 50 people, depending on the rank of the Germans harmed. Such *collective reprisals* for any act of protest took place in all cities and villages. In this manner, countless unnamed Ukrainians and Poles faced execution on the spot, or arrests and incarceration in prisons and concentration camps. The names of the first group remain mostly unknown.

I often heard it whispered that one should be wary of former communist collaborators, because such people easily switch sides and become Nazi collaborators. The saying was *"don't trust collaborators – they serve anyone"* (meaning *"once a collaborator, always a collaborator"*). Later, one of the much talked about incidents took place in Kyiv, when the Nazi regime arrested the Ukrainian poet Olena Teliha. After the Soviets retreated, some communists were given orders to stay in the city. They served, or pretended to serve, as Nazi collaborators, and it is believed that they denounced Teliha to the Nazis. The communists were given instructions to annihilate Ukrainian intellectuals; it did not matter whether a communist or a Nazi hand performed such deeds, as long as the directive to remove "the enemies of the people" was carried out. In order to leave the people without their own leaders, both the Soviets and the Nazis tried to eliminate Ukrainian cultural, intellectual, and, obviously, also political leaders.

During times of war, and especially during foreign occupations, some groups of people suffer more from one enemy, while others from another. Perhaps one cannot, and even should not, compare "who is the cruelest enemy of them all," be it Russians/communists or Germans/Nazis. Both of them brought horrific losses of life and great suffering to the peoples of modern Europe.

Both regimes decimated Europe, as they more than decimated Ukraine.

There would not have been so many victims on all sides, had the Russians and the Germans stayed within their own borders, and not coveted the territories of their neighbors.

Chapter 5

WAS I TO BE THE 6,000,001ST VICTIM?
Or
THE CASE OF THE GREY UMBRELLA WITH A WHITE CROCODILE LEATHER HANDLE

In 1939, the Halychyna (or Galicia) part of western Ukraine had a population of close to 6 million. Out of that number, almost 4 million were Ukrainians (approx. 65%), a million were Poles (16.5%), 600,000 were Jews, and 49,000 were Germans and others. But in the cities, the proportion was different. In my town, Stryi, the population of 30,000 plus, consisted of almost equal parts of Ukrainians, Poles, and Jews.

For children, access to education kept changing depending on the ruling foreign regime. In the first four grades, the education was mostly in the native language of the children, while in the secondary schools, students had to attend Polish schools with some Ukrainian courses. By 1930, the Polish administration reduced the number of Ukrainian schools, gymnasia, and teachers' seminaries to just a few, mostly private ones. As a child of 4 or 5, I played with children of different ethnic origins. I particularly remember playing with a Polish boy called Leszek, who was a neighbor.

*Photos 21-5. Leszek and his older brother Staszek,
with me in the center, on 20 Doyizdova Street*

During the Nazi/German occupation, most of the Jewish
population of Stryi was forcibly relocated to one part of the city.
It was then that I heard the word *ghetto* for the first time, and
initially did not really grasp its significance.

There were announcements all over the city forbidding non-
Jews to provide shelter to Jews, who, instead, were to live "in
specially created Jewish housing areas" of the city, i.e. the ill-
famed *ghettos. Those who provided food or shelter to Jews were to
be punished by death.*

When I was about 7 or 8 years old, one Sunday morning I was on my
way to our school, where all students and teachers usually gathered
before going to church in an organized manner; such a meeting was
called *exorta* (from the Latin, a preparatory talk). On that day I was
a little late, and as I rushed by the old Jewish quarter to get to school,
four men in uniform stopped me quite unexpectedly. Later, I learned
that two of them were Nazi Gestapo policemen, and the other two
were local Jewish militiamen (working for the *Judenrat*, or Jewish

Council, in the ghetto). The Gestapo asked me, *"Bist du eine Judin?"* [Are you Jewish?]. I knew enough German already to answer *"Ich bin eine Ukrainerin"* [I am Ukrainian]. But the Jewish militiamen kept insisting that they knew me and that I was definitely Jewish. I have no idea why the militiamen wanted to count me as a Jew; if a Jew was found outside the ghetto, a most severe punishment was handed out, quite often death.

The men in uniform started taking me with them, when a store owner, where we often shopped, Mr. Rak (I don't remember his first name), passed by. The Gestapo stopped him and demanded to see his passport; then, they asked him if he recognized me. He said that he knew my whole family, and stated my name and nationality (this was always a requirement with them). After several more exchanges of questions and answers, the Germans released me with a comment to Mr. Rak: "We filled our Ukrainian quota for the day, so you and the girl can go." That is what he related later to my parents.

This was my first brush with a threat of execution.

The next day, Mother took me to the Stryi town hall to get my very own passport with a photo. Passports stated the nationality (e.g. Ukrainian, Polish or Jewish) and religion of the holder. As we were waiting for my papers to be processed, an attorney working there, who knew my mother, came to say hello and invited us to his office, where citizens usually came for various permits. As we sat there, the man talked to us about a particular permit, and kept writing something and handing small pieces of paper to my mother, while at the same time indicating with his finger to be quiet. That attorney was aware that the Nazis listened to every word uttered there, so writing notes was the only way to communicate personal or secret information. I learned later, that in the notes, he pleaded with my mother to help another mother, who had a girl my age. He proposed a specific plan, which my mother would have to follow the following day. Mother agreed.

At the end of the meeting with the man, I received my passport and was told to carry it with me at all times. I was very proud of it; certainly none of my friends had one! On the top page, the letter "U" (for "Ukrainian") was displayed in bold print, and inside was my photograph.

The next morning, Mother unexpectedly asked if I would like to have a sister my own age. I was thrilled with the idea and eagerly replied that it was always my dream to have a sister. Mother then warned me that in order to make this happen, I had to do exactly as she would instruct me, because it was wartime and we had to be extra careful what we were doing and how. Then we left to go to a pharmacy, which stood on the corner of two streets delineating the Jewish ghetto. The pharmacy was still open to all citizens. Mother told me that once we were inside the store, I would need to take off my coat and wait until a little girl (my future sister!) would put it on, and then she was to *walk out with* my mother. I was to follow by myself, five minutes later, with no coat, but with *my passport* in my pocketbook. It was just like a weird game.

Photo 22-5. My first passport picture at 8 years of age (1943)

I was dressed in a light spring coat. Once inside the pharmacy, after Mother exchanged a few words with the pharmacist, he told her that the mother of my "future sister" came to the arranged meeting a little early and informed him that she had thought it over, and that actually she lost her nerve, and could not part with her daughter, even though it possibly meant saving her life. She was very grateful for the risk that my family took, and as a gesture of gratitude, left us a grey umbrella with a white crocodile leather handle in the shape of a fox's head. To this day, I think I can almost feel the slightly rough texture of that unusual white leather handle.

For many years, through all the strange events that World War II brought on us, somehow I was able to hold on to that umbrella from the unknown woman. And I often wondered whether her little girl managed to survive the Holocaust.

There were strict orders from the Nazis not to hide any Jews or other people for whom the Nazis were looking. The punishment was death! This would also apply to the whole *family* of the person providing shelter! It took me several decades to comprehend the risk to our whole family that my mother took in trying to save that little Jewish girl, whom we never even met, whose name we never found out. Nevertheless, my parents felt that they had to do the right thing. One of every four Ukrainian families, whom I knew, also took such risks. But there are no known records of how many were successful, how many perished for doing this, or even how many were misidentified as being Jewish, just as I was on that day.

Chapter 6

MARIA, WHO WOULDN'T BE SAVED

Uncle Lonhyn was the chief surgeon at a hospital in Sambir. Many people turned to him for help and advice, even about non-medical matters. Uncle knew that my mother was an activist in the Ukrainian Women's Organization; in our town, she was in charge of a committee helping village girls who wished to work in town as cooks, nannies, or maids. The women's society provided the young women with necessary training for such jobs, and prepared them to become good housekeepers when they married. Another important service that the society performed was ensuring that the girls were placed in safe homes, were treated properly there, knew their own rights, and knew where to turn if they needed help. One day, Uncle Lonhyn asked my mother to help Maria, the daughter of a local patient, and to find her a job as a housekeeper or maid. Since we had recently lost our maid, Mother gladly agreed to engage Maria.

I was about 7 or 8 years old then, and was not told any details about Maria's family. I liked her a lot and called her "Marusia," (a gentle diminutive of Maria), as she preferred. She often read stories to me, sang Ukrainian songs, wore blouses with Ukrainian embroidery, and regularly attended church services.

She was with us for several months, until one day she did not come home after going shopping. The following day, Mother kept asking around town whether anyone had seen her. Two young

41

women friends of Maria sadly related what they witnessed the day before. In those days, trains with boxcars often transported young people destined for forced labor (or worse) in Germany. That day, the train arrived already filled with young people from another town. As the young women and Maria were watching the train that slowed down at our train station, she suddenly shrieked that she recognized her sister on that train heading to Germany. Without giving it much thought, Maria quickly ran to the train about to depart and joined her sister. That was the last time that her friends saw her, and the last that we heard of her.

When I was older, Mother confessed that she knew from the start that Maria was Jewish, and, in order to protect her, encouraged her to assume an outward demeanor identifying herself as a Ukrainian (such as wearing an embroidered Ukrainian blouse and singing in a Ukrainian choir). Now, I marvel at the risks that my parents took in «knowingly harboring a Jew." Had Maria ever admitted who hid her, none of us would have survived. This was the *modus operandi* of the Nazis: instill fear in all who disobey, and severely punish anyone who was helping Jews or others whom the Nazis wanted to arrest or send to Germany.

In most cities in Ukraine and Poland, trains, like the one that Maria boarded, in order to be with her sister, were seen daily. Occasionally, some people were fortunate to escape from such trains. A friend, D.M., told me about her brother Z. (in the town of Zolochiv), who saw such a train with young people in it. He quickly went to the back of the cars and unbolted doors so that many people managed to escape.

Another aspect of the Nazi occupation was persecution of community and cultural leaders, as well as the clergy. Many Ukrainians and Poles were arrested and/or killed in each city and town. Besides persecution of individuals, the Nazis also pursued complete liquidation of ethnic groups: Jews and Gypsies. At that time, a variant of the Christian question "AND WHO IS MY BROTHER?" was often heard in various forms. To some, the answer came naturally, while others were inspired by the clergy's calls and example. Hundreds of Jews found a place to hide from the Nazis at the Archbishop Andrei Sheptytsky's seminary, in his own official residence in Lviv, or in other Ukrainian Greco-Catholic churches and monasteries. On 21 November 1942, the

Archbishop sent out a pastoral letter to the clergy, nuns, and the faithful asking them not to be passive bystanders to what the Nazis were doing, but to try to protect people against "political murders" and the shedding of innocent blood. The text of that letter was read in all Ukrainian Greco-Catholic churches. The Archbishop's own brother and other Ukrainian monks hid 183 Jews in their monasteries. They did this while placing their own lives at risk. I don't know whether my parents knew of the Archbishop's letter or whether they had arrived at the same decision themselves in the two situations that we faced when my family was hiding a Jew and risking a life trying to save an unknown Jewish girl.

On 3 June 1943, a notice entitled "Reminder," stated that anyone providing shelter, food, or hiding any Jews (outside the ghetto) would be punished by death. This announcement was signed by S.S. Group Commander Katzmann in the city of Lviv.

Nevertheless, many people did risk their lives, often to help complete strangers. Sadly, not all such attempts were successful, sometimes because of the impatience of the people being saved (as in the case of my "would be sister.") Our very good friends and neighbors, the Duwalos, hid two Jewish colleagues, and then one of them decided to visit his own house. Unfortunately, he was caught, and confessed where he was hiding. (In Part II, I provide more examples of those who survived.) And who knows how many individuals in Ukraine were executed for providing shelter to their Jewish friends and neighbors, or just Jewish strangers, as well as Christians who were persecuted by the Nazis. I am not aware of any statistics of these Nazi victims.

Chapter 7

AND WHERE IS MY BROTHER?

Photo 23-7. My brother Vsevolod (or Vlodko) Zalesky,
with our parents (c. 1933)

My brother Vlodko was nine years older than I. When the Nazis came, he was in what is comparable to Grade 11; he attended the Ukrainian Classical Gymnasium (high school). Over time, he was increasingly absent from home. On occasion, he would rush in, quite obviously hungry, and gobble up any available food (which was getting really scarce at the time).

By the time my brother had been away for several weeks, I no longer believed the excuses that my parents gave me, and had to ask them point blank: "Just *where is* Vlodko?" The answers were not forthcoming. Obviously, when I grew older, I forgave my parents, understanding then that children can easily disclose a secret. And the secret was that my brother was training to be in the Resistance. *He chose to be an insurgent, training to fight against the Nazis as well as the communists, both of them being foreign powers with foreign ideologies, both of them foreign invaders.*

In hindsight, Vlodko's choice was predictable, although at the time, I would not have known why exactly. About a year earlier, still during the first Soviet occupation, my grandparents sent their driver to bring us some produce and meat from the country. My brother gave the driver a letter to take back to our *Babunia*. In it, this 15-year old youngster was telling his grandmother that it was time to prepare and protect our country against foreign invaders. The KGB somehow managed to get the letter, and one evening, their representatives came to interrogate my parents, taking them to KGB headquarters. When Mother protested that she could not leave me alone (I was about 6 years old then), the KGB men pointed to their female colleague who would stay with me for the night (of course, their interrogations had to be at night!).

I remember how that woman tried very hard to play some game with me, and then attempted to tickle my feet. It was at that moment that I told myself never to admit that my feet are ticklish. And from that time on, I never strayed from that determination! That woman kept asking me weird questions about where we could hide something around the house. I had neither such information, nor any idea what to hide, nor any clue what she was talking about. There was something very unpleasant about her, even her bright and fake blond hair. I disliked her tone and behavior. I could say that I could feel in my body something wicked about her (to paraphrase Shakespeare). She certainly did not win me over, no matter how much she tried. Nor did she learn anything about my brother's "revolutionary plans," about which the other KGB agents kept asking my parents. Many years later, I learned that a couple of months before this episode with my brother, in January 1941, 59 people were tried in Lviv for treason against the USSR. Among them were several Ukrainian activists, but most were high school and college students (37 young men and 22 young women, some only

15 years old). Most of them were given death sentences. That is why the Soviets were so suspicious! They were looking for proof of some "irregular" activities among Ukrainian teenagers.

This incident with my brother took place near the end of "the First Soviet Occupation" of the western regions of Ukraine (1939-1941). It was a good indication of what would follow if the Communist regime returned, as it did for the second occupation, which lasted from 1945 to 1991.

Photo 24-7. My brother (in the middle) and his classmates in 1943

Then from 1941-1944, the Nazis came and took over from their former allies. Because of general resentment against the Nazis, obviously venues of protest had to develop, just as they did against the communists. In 1943, Ukrainian and Polish boys who reached the age of 17 to 18 received official letters from the Nazi occupation administration, directing them to register for compulsory hard labor in Germany. Ukrainians were also granted permission to organize their own military division to fight against the communists. But there was a third, voluntary, option for young men and many women (although it wasn't in that letter): to join the Resistance, in the form of the Ukrainian Partisan Army (UPA) and fight against both the communists and the Nazis. My brother chose this option, because to him, it represented an obvious hope for Ukraine's future. The young volunteers wished to protect their land from all invaders. Although young Ukrainians predominated in the UPA, there were also Jews and members of other ethnic groups. Among the Jewish volunteers, were many physicians, much needed in the underground environment of the insurgents.

(See: Aleksei S. Zheleznov, "Ievrei v ukrainskoi povstancheskoj armii (UPA)" [Jews in the Ukrainian Partisan Army]. http://grimnir74.livejournal.com/5258806.html (4 August, 2016, 9:00).

Photo 25-7. Ukrainian Resistance forces (UPA) arresting Nazi soldiers

By spring 1945, the Ukrainian insurgents had more volunteers than their partisan army was able to arm and shelter in the forests (large numbers of Soviet deserters were also joining them), so many of the youngest men were discharged. Then, after the Nazis were defeated, the UPA had only one front to fight, against the Soviets. But how long could they last, hiding in forests? Small groups managed to last well into the 1950s.

The question "Where is my brother?" haunted me for a long time after we left Ukraine, although I understood very well that the border (later called the Iron Curtain), separating free Europeans from the communist world, prevented us from getting news directly from home. When we were in Western Europe, I remember looking at strangers who were only slightly similar to him, thinking perhaps that man could be my brother? I had greater hope when we learned that the UPA had sent over a couple hundred members to Western Europe specifically to "let the world know about Ukraine's predicament." There was an incident in 1947, while we were in the Neu-Ulm Displaced Persons camp, that I heard someone call a man "Mr. Zalesky."

I rushed over immediately and asked the man what his first name was (even though he did not look much like my brother). It wasn't him! But I kept on hoping and looking. It almost became an obligatory game with me: if I saw a young man whom I liked, I kept asking myself "*what if* he were my brother?" Later, in my adult life, I had several very good male friends in whom I had no romantic interest, but whom I probably subconsciously considered as substitutes for my brother.

It was not until much later that we learned my brother's fate. When he and several of his colleagues were released from the UPA, they still wished to serve the people, and chose to do it as priests. They turned to Archbishop Sheptytsky to accept them to his seminary. He did. But he died on November 1, 1944, and several months later the Ukrainian Greco-Catholic Church was banned by the Soviets. In March 1946, the Soviet regime called for a Synod (assembly or conference) of Ukrainian Greco-Catholic priests, who were directed to revoke the 1595 Union of Brest (Union with the Catholic Church) and were forced to become part of the Russian Orthodox Church. At the same time, the Greco-Catholic seminarians were drafted into the Red Army. Because of his "past" (i.e. the theological seminary), my brother had to serve a prolonged tour of duty of six years. After his discharge, he studied medicine in Lviv. But then, when he was in his fourth

Photo 26-7. My brother's funeral in Lviv, attended by a very large group of his friends and classmates from the medical college

year of medical school, he was killed on 2 January 1955. Family members were not allowed to visit him on his deathbed in the city hospital: armed men in uniform were blocking access to him. Typical of the Soviet regime: never admit anything.

To the Soviets, Ukrainians were no allowed any religion that wasn't Russian Orthodox. As the Russians did not tolerate Ukrainian Catholics in 1783, when they drove my ancestors to flee to the western region of Ukraine, and centuries later, the communists brought about my Grandfather's death in 1941, so they also brought about my brother's death in 1955.

Photo 27-7. My brother Vlodko (1926-1955) in 1951, when he was a medical student in Lviv

We don't often realize how the global aspects of war, as well as the various peace treaties that end them, force themselves into people's individual lives. Who would have thought that the fate of a 21-year-old Ukrainian man in Ukraine would be influenced by how an American President (in this case, President Roosevelt) voted at the Yalta Conference in February of 1945?

First of all, it was in Yalta that Churchill and Roosevelt agreed to hand over Western Ukraine to Stalin, i.e. be part of the Soviet Union. Secondly, President Roosevelt made known his interest in the Kurile Islands (the islands just north of Japan). The U.S.

wanted to have its own bases in the Far East, to be ready in case of a continued armed conflict with Japan. Therefore, at the Yalta Conference, the U.S. voted to support Russia's/USSR's claim to the Kurile Islands (except for the two southernmost large islands), rather than let Japan continue its ownership (which had been won from Imperial Russia in 1904-1905). These islands were barren and rocky, and had severely cold and stormy winters; it is for this reason that they were considered to be one of the worst assignments for Soviet soldiers. It was there, on the Urup Island, that my brother was stationed for 6 years. The Soviets occupied these islands on 1 September 1945. After the USSR was dissolved in 1991, Russia took over control of the northern islands.

In his letters from the Far East to his Aunt Daria, Vlodko sometimes described the rough landscape, the terrible cold climate, and usually ended his narrative with a Soviet soldier's obligatory text of this nature:

"...We need to over fulfill the norms of Stalin's Five-Year Plan. As soldiers of the Far East, we are here on a special mission, we guard the borders of our fatherland in particularly taxing circumstances dealing with the climate, etc. The Party and the government value this especially, and they value highly [those of us] who serve in the Far East...
I wish you all good health, my respects to Uncle and kisses to [my cousins] Roksoliana and Dzvinka!
I kiss your hand, Vsevolod."

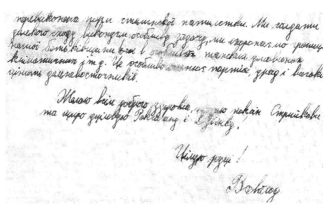

Photo 28-7. From a letter, written in Ukrainian to Aunt Daria
(Uncle Stefan's wife), on 12 February 1948

No wonder that the obligation to write such propagandistic phrases brought about his contemplation on truth, as in the following letter.

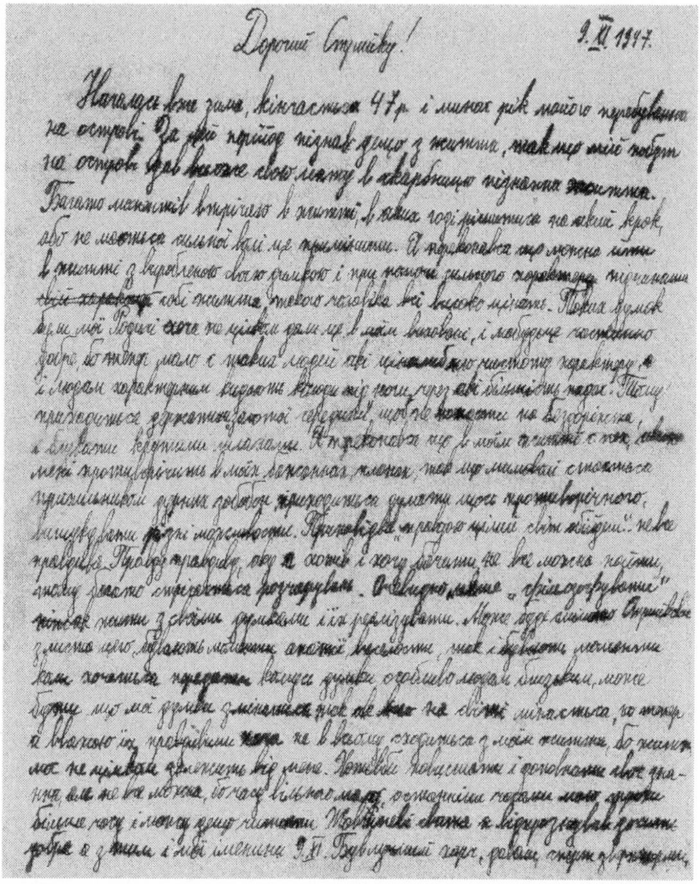
Дорогий Стрийку! 9.XI.1947.

Почалася вже зима, кінчається 47 р. і минає рік мойого перебування на острові.

Photo 29-7. Vlodko's letter, written in Ukrainian, to Uncle Stefan

[Dear Uncle! 9 November 1947

Winter has begun, and the year 1947 is ending, as does a whole year of my life spent on this island. During this time, I learned something about life, therefore my presence on the island has made a contribution into the treasure chest of my knowledge of life. There were quite a few moments in my life when it wasn't easy to make a decision which path to choose, or there was not enough willpower to put this into practice. I came to the conclusion that one goes into life with a chosen idea, and then with the help of a strong character, makes life follow that path; people value such individuals. I think that my parents thought so too, although they didn't fully insist on this in my upbringing; that was probably for the better, since nowadays there are very few people who value purity in a character. Such people get all kinds of logs thrown under their feet, and because of this, majority of people fall. It is for this reason that people often prefer to stick to the golden middle, rather than find themselves with no roads to choose from, and be forced to go astray along twisted paths.

I see, that in my life, there is a jinx acting contrary to my wishes and plans. This almost makes me ready to rely on a silly superstition: think the opposite of what you wish for. The proverb "With truth, you can go around the whole world and come back, too," does not always hold true. It isn't always possible to find a true truth, something that I personally wanted and still want to see, and that is why one meets with many disappointments. Obviously, it is easier to philosophize than to follow one's ideas and see them come to life. Uncle, you may laugh at this letter, as it demonstrates my moments of apathy, as well as of joyfulness, or moments when I need to share my thoughts, especially with people who are close to me. Perhaps my ideas will change, as everything changes in this world, but at this moment, I consider them to be true. However, my life does not seem to reflect all of them, since my life does not completely depend upon me. [...]

On November 9th, I celebrated my name day [St. Vsevolod's Day] [...]

Vlodko]
(when he was 21 years old)

He wrote this letter to Uncle Stefan, who was a lawyer in the city of Lviv, and Vlodko's Godfather. He and his family were the substitute family for Vlodko when he had no news about our parents and me in the West (it is very likely that he didn't even know whether we were alive, and it was only in the late 1950s that our relatives in Ukraine heard indirectly about our survival). His references to chosen paths in life may refer to his dream to serve his country, either in the resistance, or as a priest, or a physician.

This was the *first log under his feet* (his reference to the logs, above). He served in the resistance for about a year (at the age of 18 to 19); then, many younger men were released from the formation. Next came his choice to study theology and become a Greco-Catholic priest. This status couldn't be achieved either. This *was the second log* along his path.

Some ex-theologians were given a chance to prove themselves as Soviet citizens. They were drafted into the Red Army, and sent to the most challenging assignment on the barren, formerly Japanese, Kurile Islands. Rather than the usual three years of duty, Vlodko's term was doubled – *the third log along his path.*

Photo 30-7. The only recreation on the Kurile Islands that the soldiers could find was playing in a military band. Vlodko played on the big tuba (last row, on the right); as a youngster, he played on the piano quite well, and thus easily picked up playing another instrument in the Far East.

Later, upon his return from the Red Army, he passed the required high school equivalency examinations, and was accepted into medical school in Lviv. Four years later, *the biggest and final log along his path* was the one that crushed his life at the age of 28.

Chapter 8

WAR YEARS, LEAN YEARS

The war's presence was felt in many aspects of our family's private life. Not only food was in short supply, but clothes as well. I remember the specific problem of clothing when I was to have my First Holy Communion, in 1943. We could not buy a white dress, and had to borrow one from a friend. Similarly, white shoes, stockings, and gloves were not available in stores. My short veil was cut from a long one that was my mother's wedding veil.

This situation during WWII could not even compare to the one during World War I, when my mother and her sister received their First Holy Communion.

In comparing daily life during WWI and WWII in the same setting, what a difference there was in the availability of items for daily use. White shoes were not the only scarce item during the

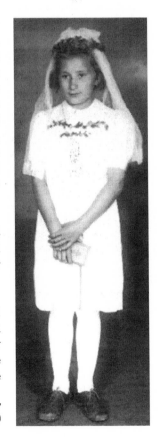

Photo 31-8. Getting ready for my First Holy Communion during WWII (1943)

Photo 32-8. First Holy Communion during World War I:
Aunt Stysia and my mother

Nazi occupation; so were regular shoes of any color, and even shoelaces. I recollect an incident with them.

One morning, the day did not start well for me. For some reason I had to hurry while dressing. When I got to the shoes, I remembered that one of my shoelaces had torn the day before, and so now I would not be able to tie the shoe. Ever since I turned 8 years old, Mother insisted that I always get my dress and shoes ready the night before. And I always did that, except on this one occasion. But shoelaces were not easy to get during the war and had to be handled with care. I could not ask our housekeeper/ maid, Maria, to help me (although she offered). I had to take care of the problem myself. In those days, electrical wires for household purposes (for lamps and radios) were encased in a thin knitted fabric that served as a coating or insulation and looked like a "stocking" for the wires. On Mother's suggestion, I found a piece of unused wire, cut the necessary length, and then pulled out the wire from that "stocking." I was left holding a rather respectable-looking brown shoelace. Problem solved! I laced my shoes, tied my brown shoelaces, and rushed to town.

In the summer of 1942 or 1943, I went to stay with Uncle Yakiv and Aunt Kazia again for several weeks. Mother and I packed my clothes. But there was a problem with shoes. They were scarce even in shoe stores. Mother managed to get the last lovely pair of Mary-Jane shoes in size 34, and packed them in my suitcase. At first when I was at my Uncle's, I wore my sandals. My Aunt had a seamstress make me a striking summer dress (navy georgette with red lining) for going visiting or to church; the dress certainly required a new pair of navy or patent leather shoes. When I tried the pair that Mother bought me, only the right shoe fit, while the left was far too small. So Auntie took me shopping in Kopychyntsi, where she knew the owner of a good shoe store.

My Uncle and Aunt had no children and enjoyed showering me with attention and gifts. On that visit, Auntie bought me a great-looking pair of patent leather shoes. I tried them on, and they fit me perfectly. Several weeks later, we were going to a birthday party and I was to wear my best outfit. The dress looked perfect, the shoes looked great with it, but there was a little problem with my left shoe: I couldn't uncurl my toes in it. Again, I was left with only the right shoe! What a situation! And the store was all out of a larger size. Apparently, my left foot grew first or faster, and during wartime, shoe stores were short on selection.

In addition to such scarcities in clothing and shoes, there were extensive food shortages, especially more prominent in the larger towns and cities. Uncle Yakiv lived in a more rural setting, and was a landowner himself. In the spring of 1942 or 1943, the River Stryi flooded its embankments, and the floodwaters ruined many nearby farms. As a result, in our hometown, produce was scarce, and whatever did exist, the Nazis took. For some reason, Aunt Kazia asked my mother to send her a new scale. Mother bought a scale, packed it, and told me to write a note about it to my Aunt. Auntie asked me to always be very specific when I had a request, and I promised her that I would. So I took the initiative to add my own list of food items that we lacked and would appreciate. I was probably not very subtle about it, because Mother would not let me post that letter.

The Nazis were requisitioning most of the produce and meat from Ukrainian farmers in order to send it all to Germany or to the front, and so very little was left for the local population in towns or cities. All produce and groceries were harder and harder to get, and sugar was particularly scarce during the war years. People tried to find decent substitutes: cook sugar beets until enough of the sweet mass would solidify. I remember my brother suggesting that we place one small cube of sugar on the table, and look at it intently while sipping our cups of tea, all the time imagining that the sugar is actually *in* our cups. Treats were also rare, and what we substituted for them was very modest, though still very tasty to us at the time: for example, very thin slices of a peeled potato, with a few grains of salt added, were roasted on top of the range; they tasted as quite a delicacy! It was then that I learned that we could plant potatoes without giving up the whole potato: you just had to cut the peel with one node on it, and plant just that tiny piece. A potato plant would grow just the same. And then, a potato in any form or shape would taste heavenly with a few grains of salt (I discovered quite unexpectedly that I loved salt as much as sugar, and could eat a teaspoonful at a sitting).

Since hardly any desserts or even treats were available, another story remains strongly etched in my mind. Mother had a good friend, Mrs. Mykolayevych, (Mrs. M.), who during "the good old days" (prewar times) was known for baking the most delicious tortes ever. To be invited to her Sunday tea was an event in itself at any time, and during the food shortage especially so. How she managed to adjust her recipes to the available meager food products was a case of artistry and magic. Mrs. M. always loved a touch of mystery; even in the prewar days, she would not allow her cook to observe her when she baked her tortes, so that no one would know her personal recipes. There were stories about other ladies trying to entice Mrs. M's cooks with promises of outlandish wages. But it didn't work, since the cooks didn't know her recipes!

I have no idea how Mrs. M. managed to get any ingredients for a cake during the Soviet and Nazi occupations. One Sunday, we attended her tea, and she served a super-delicious torte (I had a sweet tooth!). After everyone had a nice slice, and the obligatory one piece was left on the rotating cake stand, there was some kind of commotion when everyone's attention was focused on the glass doors leading to the garden. At that moment, I took the initiative and quickly grabbed that last piece. These days, who knew when I would get another chance like that? *Forget etiquette! Act now, or never hold such a treat in my mouth again*, I thought. It's wartime, after all! I ate it quickly, while all the guests chuckled at this with kind understanding when they turned to look at the table. The memory of this event caused endless embarrassment for me when I met any of them years later.

During 1941-43, the Nazi army had priority in terms of all types of food (from dairy, to produce, and meat), next on the list was the Nazi administration in town, and only then the local population. However, the farmers whose children went to high school in the city, obviously had better access to produce, and thus many people in Stryi (and probably in other cities as well) were forced to rent rooms to such students, whose parents then paid with produce. One day, a woman (whose name we never learned) came to our house and said that she knew that my father was a teacher who was highly respected, and that it hurt her to know that many types of produce and dairy were not available to us at the time. She gave my mother a pound of butter, some dried mushrooms, and a jar of jam. When Father heard about this kind gesture, he asked Mother to give away these precious items to an orphanage and never accept gifts from parents of any students, so there would be no impropriety, nor even an appearance of a possible impropriety between a student's family and that of a teacher and his family.

Obviously, buying produce in a large city was much harder (or even impossible) than in a town surrounded by villages. My father's brother Stefan and his family lived in Lviv (which is 10 times larger than Stryi). One day I was walking home with my girlfriends, when a couple blocks away from our street we saw a beautiful middle-aged woman with a knapsack on her back, holding by the hand two girls, aged four and five years old. When we were close to our church, the lady stopped us and asked for directions to Lelewel Street. I offered to guide her, and very soon we both discovered that she was my Aunt Daria, and the girls were my cousins, whom I had never met. In desperation that produce and meat were so scarce in Lviv, they made the trip by train, hoping that my parents would be able to help them buy some. After that visit, I didn't complain about not having any delicacies or even some staple foods. At least my parents did not have to travel to another city to look for food.

Facing food shortages lead many a family in the city to keep one or two hens. So did my family. We got a red one and a black one, and kept them in the corner of our wood shed. I have no idea whether it was legal or not, but these two cute hens provided us with two eggs a day, and thus contributed to a tremendous improvement in our nutrition.

In regard to food scarcity (especially meat), I remember another incident that was widely talked about with obvious glee. During the Nazi occupation, farm animals were registered and each one of them had to be regularly accounted for (each animal was given a numbered metal earpiece). It was next to impossible to find a piglet that the inspectors had missed, and under threat of death, no one would dare to cheat the Nazi authorities in this! However, two local daredevils were able to buy or steal an unregistered pig, which somehow had to be transported to the city. The men decided to dress the pig as an old granny in glasses, with a large hat covering the face, and booties on its legs. They pulled the pig along, just as if they were walking arm-in-arm with a slightly tipsy person, and then took their seats on a train. I don't remember how this adventure ended, but the fact that people were so ingenious and tried to outwit the Nazis was not only funny, but also somehow very uplifting. No wonder this story made the rounds all over the country.

Chapter 9

WHY WERE ALL THE REGIMES
AFRAID OF YOUNG SCOUTS?

Ukrainian Plast Scouting was organized in 1911 and flourished until 1930, when the Polish administration banned it. Then, in 1939-41 and after 1945, the Soviets would not even consider allowing organizations that were not initiated by them. The Nazi regime in 1942, behaved similarly. However, representatives of the underground Ukrainian Scouting were able to organize an educational society for the young, called VSUM (Ukrainian Youth Educational Society). By somehow managing to get around the Nazi prohibition of Scouting, the new organization provided an opportunity for youngsters at least to attend summer camps.

In the summer of 1943, I had a chance to go, for several weeks, to a Ukrainian summer camp. Although I had been away from my family before (staying with my grandparents or one of my aunts and uncles), this was my first summer camp, so I felt very grown up.

The camp was held near the River Stryi, in the town of Korchyn, in the Carpathian Mountains. Closer to the river, was a camp for girls, while the one for boys was in the town, allowing both groups to hold morning and evening prayers together. Since the Nazis not only did not allow Scouting uniforms and insignias, or scouting programs, but obviously, even the Ukrainian name for Scouting ("Plast"), therefore, we had to take advantage of what was available.

Photo 33-9. Ukrainian youth summer camp in Korchyn, 1943

We enjoyed new friends and camp life itself. To many city kids it was also a great adventure to see the Carpathians Mountains and go on field trips and excursions. During the war years, few of us could purchase appropriate camp outfits, so we wore our city clothes.

Photo 34-9. A field trip (I am in the first row, first on the right)

Scouting and summer camps used to be different a dozen years or so earlier. During the 1920s, Ukrainian Scouts were allowed to wear uniforms and were a legal organization. My father served as the Gymnasium counselor and advisor to Ukrainian Scouts in the city of Sambir (1913-20) and then in Stryi (1926-30).

Photo 35-9. My father, in the white hat, with his group of students from two upper grades

It saddened me that although I was old enough to join Scouting, I was not able to be a Brownie. Since I had no choice, I tried to enjoy the substitute camp in Korchyn as much as possible.

One day, we went hiking up a mountain called Konyk, covered with bushes of wild blueberries. I was so happy to be able to pick them myself and eat them fresh from the bush. I wanted to bring some back to camp for snacking. But I had no paper bags or containers for them. I decided to use my hankie (a girl should always have a nice hankie in her pocket!) to hold them. It did not take long for the blueberries to disappear into my mouth, while the proof of my "misdemeanor" remained on the hankie: no matter how many times I washed it, the dark purple-and-blue stains remained there forever. In a way, it was a good lesson about natural food coloring, as well as a nice memento of that hike.

Since the unofficial underground scouting somehow managed to exist during the Nazi regime, my brother was able to participate in it. In 1943, during Holy Friday and Saturday, his troop volunteered to keep vigil at Christ's symbolic tomb in our church. Such practices were not allowed during the two years of the Soviet rule, so young Scouts were happy to be involved in Christian programs again. The young men (15-17) who volunteered for this duty had to take turns standing guard for 30-minute periods, round-the-clock. Since they were not allowed to wear Scout uniforms, instead, they wore traditional Ukrainian folk outfits. I remember how uplifted my brother and his friends were when they described that they had to sleep at the rectory, because their turns would come up every two hours or so. They admired our young and congenial parish priest, Rev. Artemiy Tsehelsky, and were most appreciative that he and his wife took care of them, providing them dinner, breakfast, and snacks while the boys took their turns on the guard duty.

Chapter 10

JUST A TEMPORARY FAREWELL
TO UKRAINE?

One day in at the beginning of July 1944, during the Nazi occupation, I was playing in the courtyard, when suddenly I heard sounds of an airplane flying low and shooting, rather than dropping bombs. The closest structure to which I could run was the laundry and storage hut in the courtyard. As I tried to reach it, I saw the silvery wings of the plane and then felt something scraping my leg. After I was safely in the hut, I noticed blood running down the back of my left leg; upon examination, I concluded that some kind of shrapnel must have scratched me. Yes, now I was really convinced that war was heating up again, and the front lines were closing in on us.

The following day, people described that plane as British. It is quite possible that it was a British Air Force plane helping out the Soviets, who were now pushing west again. The significance of the plane was painfully obvious: with the front line approaching, so were the Russians. It was then that my parents decided to prepare to leave the city in order to be in some more rustic and hilly surroundings during the worse days of the front line. We gathered some of our most necessary items, and transported them by train to a rented cottage in the mountains, near the town of Sanok (across the border in Poland). We were going to take a train to get there just before the frontline would be getting close.

Suddenly the Germans were retreating and taking local people with them. It was on 24 July 1944, that we were forced to leave our hometown, Stryi. We had about 10 minutes to grab whatever we could, and were put in army trucks. (I managed to quickly take my two angora rabbits and leave them with the neighbors.) Each of us had a knapsack and a suitcase. While we threw into them some unnecessary items that we chose rather hastily, nevertheless we somehow managed to take a few rather important ones, too: photographs, as well as documents, several books. We also grabbed various papers, many of them rather purposeless: telegrams and greeting cards sent to my parents on their wedding day in 1924! While my parents were hoping that somehow we would be able to get to Sanok, apparently that was not to be, because the Russians were already there.

Somewhere down the road, where trains were still running, we were put on a freight car. There were about a dozen other families in our car. For, what seemed like a couple of days, our train would shuffle a few miles at a time, and then would stop. The train was also getting longer, with several boxcars added here and there. Not only did most of us have very limited possessions, we had very little food supplies. The main concern was that no matter where the train took us, we only wished that it would go *west*, as far as possible from the approaching Russian communists and the terror that they would bring again.

On that journey to who-knows-where, two specific moments remain vivid in my mind. One took place when I was looking through the open door of the boxcar, and suddenly saw a sign with the word "BORDER" in several languages. I asked my mother, "What does that really mean?" Mother replied, "It means that we are leaving Ukrainian territory." This seemed like a simple observation or statement of fact, but I reacted with shouts of protest. I did not wish to leave Ukraine! My verbalized reaction, in turn, also brought a sudden outburst of tears and deep sighing from the adults, as they faced the realization that we were now *homeless refugees*, separated from our country by cruel historical events. We had no roof over our heads, and we didn't even know where we were being taken.

Three and a half years later, in my Grade VII composition class, I described that moment, calling it "The Saddest Day of My Life"

(see below). There were millions like me who were now refugees –
just because two large countries decided to occupy our country.

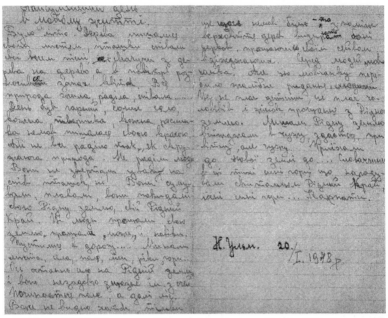

*Photo 36-10. My composition assignment, written in Ukrainian,
on 20 January 1948*

[Translation:
The Saddest Day of My Life.

*It was summer. Trees displayed their leaves, and birds sang their
joyful songs, while leaping from tree to tree. A pleasant fragrance
of flowers disseminated through the air. The surrounding nature
was alive, happy, and singing. The day was lovely, the sun was
shining, each animal and each plant looked as if it were showing
off its beauty.*

*But not everyone was as joyful as the surrounding nature: the people
were not! They did not pay any attention to the singing of the birds,
no! The people were sad, the people were shedding tears, because they
were leaving their native land, their own dear country. These people
were saying farewell to their country, perhaps even forever. They
dared to begin this journey... They passed towns, villages, fields,
forests, rivers, and mountains. Then, they reached the last village*

in their own country. That village, too, shall soon disappear from their view. Then, a different field and a different forest appeared. No houses are visible anymore, only some whiteness manages to shine through the treetops: it is the illumination of church cupolas saying farewell to the departing people.

But the people are silent. Suddenly, a mournful and sorrowful human wailing interrupts the silence. It is not the weeping of a child, only the lament of men and women, parting with their native land. They are leaving their country and entering a strange and foreign one, even though it appears friendly, still it is a foreign land. They arrive in Slovakia, a land with quiet blue mountaintops, which reminded the refugees of their own dear country, and their own blue mountains, the Carpathian Mountains.

Neu-Ulm, 20 January 1948]

The other unforgettable moment happened two borders and several months later, on 7 November 1944, when we were in Austria. One late afternoon, a small plane circled above our transport train, dropping leaflets with the shocking news that several days earlier (on 1 November 1944), Major Archbishop Andrei Sheptytsky of Lviv (Head of the Ukrainian Greco-Catholic Church) had died. This too, distressed the grieving people very deeply, since there had always been a lingering hope that he would somehow manage to protect and save us, as he had saved so many Jews a few months earlier.

Again, I could hear the collective pain expressed in the sobs of the 45 people in the freight car.

There didn't seem to be a schedule for the train stops at all, indicating when or for how long they would be. Not only that, no one even knew where the train was heading. We just hoped that the general direction would be far away from the Russians. From time to time the train would stop, since the locomotive needed to be refilled with coal and water. Our own food supplies were decreasing dangerously. The only way to get more food was to buy, or rather trade something, at an unexpected stop. The refugees who had more experience riding on such trains (i.e. those who had traveled on this train longer than we) were expert at making use of every second at any sudden stop, since they had learned survival skills and secrets much earlier.

Families needed to work as teams, and duties had to be assigned ahead of any stop. For each small group or family, one person had to run and collect several large stones to serve as sides for a pit oven; another person had to search the area for pieces of wood, while a third one would look for water. Then after lighting a fire, whatever containers or empty cans were on hand, they would serve as pots for boiling water to make coffee, tea, even soup. The most experienced and ingenious among us, who somehow found a piece of tin that could serve as a baking sheet, were able to quickly set up some type of an outdoor stove with two large stones or bricks. And then, they took that precious tin to be used at the next stop. Some people were even able to obtain a great treasure: flour! After trading some jewelry with the locals for a pound of flour, they could now fry pancakes, the greatest delicacy in this situation.

But not everyone was successful in the on-the-spot culinary art. A colleague of my father from Stryi, Professor Soltys and his family (his wife and two children who were in their late teens), were with us in the same freight car. On one of those unannounced stops, while his family was preparing a meal, Professor Soltys went to get water for cooking and washing. He was dressed only in a T-shirt and pants; he threw a towel on his shoulder, and took no wallet, nor any identification papers. But hardly a minute after he left, the train unexpectedly started to move. Everyone who was trying to cook something had to run to the cars; the family of Professor S. kept calling him, but he was nowhere nearby. They hoped that at least he would make it to the last boxcar. But he didn't! The train left, and the professor was never heard of again.

Soon we crossed another border, and were shuffled from town to town in Slovakia; at first, we stopped briefly in Banska Bystrica, and then in Krupina. It was early September 1944. Initially, all the refugees from our train were housed in a school building. Obviously, everyone was pretty hungry. One day, we were in the schoolyard, looking through the fence at the local people, while they in turn looked at us with great interest. It almost felt like being on the inside of a zoo. In our group, there was a pretty girl my age, with long blond curls and wearing a very cute dress. She drew the attention of many people on the "outside," and they soon started bringing her irresistible Kaiser rolls (with ham and cheese, at that!) and fresh fruit. When an ice-cream truck went by, several of the onlookers rushed to purchase ice-cream cones – and always gave them to her, while the rest of us kids just hungrily looked on.

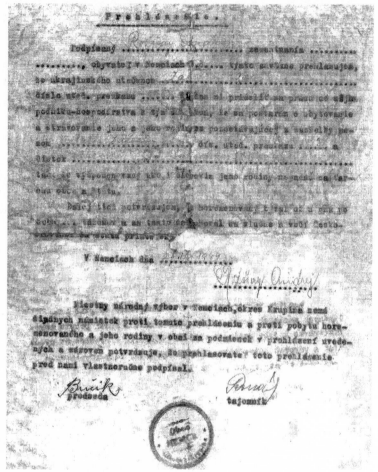

Photo 37-10. A notarized I.D. from the Slovak town Nemce

After a while, Father went to town trying to sell a piece of jewelry in order to have money for some bread. He came back very proud, since he was able to purchase three loaves of bread for a golden ring with a sapphire in it. Mother was glad for the bread, but said that next time, she should be the one to try her luck selling our jewelry. Fortunately, the next day, a local man, who was a former student of my father's, happened to hear about Ukrainian refugees there, and by chance, saw my father. The man then brought us food and even gave us some money. What a kind and considerate human being, I thought! There were several similar occurrences over the next three years. I was very proud that Father elicited such kind thoughts and deeds in his former students, obviously because they thought highly of him.

Soon, our transport with over 40 people was sent to the village of Nemce in Slovakia. Every time we came to a new city or town, we had to register as refugees with the local city hall or police, and get a permit to stay in the area.

A local farmer would need to sign an affidavit that he can provide room and board for our family, and thus we would not be a burden to the village or the country. This document then had to be countersigned by the local county committee, stating they did not object to the above arrangement (see letter below about staying in the village of Nemce).

12.septembra 1944.

Číslo: 2403/1944.

L e g i t i m a c i a .

Ukrajinskí utečenci: Zaleskyj Todij čis.leg.1585, ⬛⬛⬛.-
⬛⬛⬛ čis.leg.1103, ⬛⬛⬛ čis.leg.:1652,
⬛⬛⬛ čis.1624 ⬛⬛⬛.leg.1625, ⬛⬛⬛
⬛⬛⬛ čis.leg.4093 cestujú vlakom z Nemiec do Krupiny pre potraviny,menovite pre chlieb k pekárovi G.Benkovi do Krupiny. Legitimácia táto stráca platnosť dňom 12.sept.1944.

ved.notár

Photo 38-10. Slovak permit to take the train / shuttle to the city of Krupina, to buy bread (at G. Benko's bakery) and other products. The permit was for my father plus 5 other people, whose names I redacted (since I did not have their, or their families', permission to publish them).

71

We needed permits to shop for food, or to work on Slovak farms, allowing us to earn enough food for a few weeks—until a new instruction would arrive as to what to do with us. For example, on 21 September 1944, an order came from someone that the refugees had to leave town that very evening.

In his diary, Father noted our constant travels rather elliptically:

22ⁿᵈ: left in the afternoon. 45 people in the freight car.
23ʳᵈ arrived in Zwolene
24ᵗʰ and 25ᵗʰ in Zwolene
25ᵗʰ left for Dubrawa. Returned to Zwolene. At night arrived in Plashowa.

This was typical of our back-and-forth meanderings by train in Slovakia, Austria, and Germany during wartime in 1944-45.

In August 1944, in Banska Bystrica and the adjacent area, there was a Slovak uprising with the participation of Russian communist partisans, while a pro-German faction held the city of Bratislava. Slovaks at first preferred to support the Russians. Many Slovaks were "useful idiots," as some Russians called their ideological "fellow travellers," who soon came to see the real side of such "brothers Slavs."

The Slovak people were generally very friendly towards the Ukrainian refugees, although they could not understand why we were fleeing from the Russians, who were a Slavic people, as were: Bulgarians, Belarusians, Croats, Czechs, Macedonians, Poles, Serbs, Slovaks, Slovenes/Slovenians, and Ukrainians. Nevertheless, the Slovaks soon caught on.

Chapter 11

TWO MORE EXECUTION ATTEMPTS

A Slovak schoolhouse again provided shelter to several families, this time in the village of Nemce. Two large classrooms were cleared of desks so that the refugees could sleep on the floor. Each family slept on blankets or pieces of clothing that they had with them.

I remember a very unusual event there. I was able to pinpoint the dates thanks to my father's notebook. On 13 September 1944, the wife of the Slovak school principal gathered several girls my age (eight to ten years old) and asked for our help to pick some flowers. She wanted us to help her decorate a new "sleeping place" (i.e. two blankets and a pillow) for our neighbors. I remember a young man with blond hair (Mr. Potichnyi), unexpectedly announcing that he was marrying his sweetheart (Miss N.). The couple did not wish to risk being separated by some unfortunate war event and decided to tie the knot as soon as possible. The marriage ceremony took place in the evening, in a local Slovak church. The couple's "honeymoon suite" was on the floor of the schoolroom that five other families shared. The best that could be done for the newlyweds was to decorate their bed with freshly picked flowers. However, immediately after the ceremony, the principal and his wife announced that as a gift to the couple, they were offering their own guest room to them for the night. Still, the other girls and I were glad that the newlyweds had such a colorful "bed of flowers" for the following couple of nights.

In the meantime, the political situation and the local regime changed so often that it was hard to tell who was in charge at a particular time. Apparently, even before the Soviet communists crossed into Slovakia, Russian partisans began to appear in that area. They tried to convince Slovaks to join the communist movement and to trust them, since they too were Slavs, and thus unlike the Nazis. Those Slovaks who joined the partisans were then under pressure to get more "volunteers." The partisans would come to us, refugees, at night and pressure men to join the movement, and then threaten them with repercussions if people refused. This took place on 7 September 1944, as well as on other days (as noted in my father's diary). Occasionally, someone would warn us about such "inspections" 10 or 20 minutes ahead of time.

No one ever knew what would make the partisans dissatisfied with any person or item. My parents did not know whether it was wise to let the communist partisans (who often had little education) see our documents, especially university diplomas. Mother found a piece of sack canvas and made a large pillowcase (about 10" by 16") for our documents. Then my parents suggested that I adopt it as a "mattress" for my doll, which was just about the right height to be laid down comfortably on it. During our many months of life as refugees on the road, my dear run-down doll served us several times in many unusual situations.

Typical for the communists, the partisans usually came when it grew dark outside. Once again, a Slovak communist partisan came during the night, stating that he had orders from the Russians to eliminate all Ukrainians by the morning. At first, the Ukrainian refugee families were quite shaken, and then exploded with cries. The partisan mellowed slightly and said that he would take only men and women. Again – shattering sobs. Then he backed down and said, "Alright, just the men, then!" Women and children continued to plead. Mrs. B. pushed her children forward and said, "Beg the man for mercy!" While I stood there frozen, her children (Lida and Ihor) went down on their knees and kissed the man's hand and hugged his boots. He softened, saying that he had children too, but that he had to obey orders. Then, he advised the men to hide in the forest, while the women were to pretend to be local Slovak residents and seek housing with individual farmers. The next morning, a young man of thirty-something, with curly blond hair, dared to come back to see to his young bride; but he came disguised as a woman! I remember his unruly curly hair, which slipped out from under a kerchief. *This was a second execution attempt.*

On the whole, the Slovaks were very kind people. Many farmers gave us food and shelter in exchange for working on their farms. But the political situation kept shifting: one day there were communists, and the next day there were German tanks. On 11 October 1944, we were told to put our belongings on a freight train in the evening, and be ready to leave in the morning. My parents brought our luggage there. Then at 11 pm, a communist partisan came knocking on the window. Fearing a repetition of the previous partisan visit, Mother was so upset that she had a cardiac incident. When morning came, she was in no shape to get on the train. Father had to quickly unload our luggage and seek medical help for Mother.

By evening, we heard very sad news: the train left in the morning and had to pass through a tunnel, which happened to be mined with explosives. Hardly anyone survived. No one knew which political side was responsible for the explosives. Had it not been for Mother's heart problem, we would have been on that train, too.

The Soviets crossed into eastern Slovakia on 14 October 1944. Soviet communists and soldiers were generally called "Russians", since in the Soviet Army they all had to speak Russian, and obey Moscow's orders. As the war's front line was getting closer, so did various groups representing opposing forces: communist partisans, Russian/Soviet advancing troops, and the retreating Nazi forces. Then different flags would show up on public buildings within a day or two: the Nazi flag with a swastika, or the red communist flag, or the white-blue-and-red flag of communist Czechoslovakia. From fear, Slovak communist partisans were obeying Russian orders, and were enlisting more "volunteers" from among the young male refugees. Some, who did not comply, were often shot or hanged on the spot. The Russians particularly disliked refugees from the western parts of Ukraine, who were first occupied in 1914-1915, and then by the Soviets in 1939-1941(and proved to be quite rebellious), while most Ukrainians had experienced them since 1920, and appeared to them to be more submissive (especially after the Holodomor).

It did not take the Slovaks long to see through the Soviet propaganda. On 1 November 1944, together with about thirty other Ukrainian refugees, we were put on a freight car on the way to Bratislava. Before reaching this capital of Slovakia, we were stranded at some small rail stop, together with several other trains. Around 5 p.m., everyone from our train was ordered to leave all our belongings and assemble near the front of the train, and then cross to the next track. There we found another freight train; we could see the doors of all the cars wide open, and on the floor were strewn clothes, loaves of bread, fruit, paper money, and passports. Ominous.

At the same time, in the nearby woods, we could hear shots: rah-tah-ta-taah...

Immediately, all of us grew tense. Several Russian soldiers told us: "Don't worry. In an hour or so, you will not need to worry about anything anymore." But while these men were ordering us to get in line and follow them to the woods, an officer came and told them, "Enough for the day!"

And so, we were ordered back to our train for the night.

We survived another threat of execution.

The refugees, as well as the locomotive engineer, were firmly instructed to stay on the train. Obviously, hardly anyone slept during the night. From time to time, someone from the next car would creep in and whisper something. Suddenly, around 3 a.m., the train started moving and then frantically increased its speed. After an hour or so, it was clear that the whole train full of refugees had escaped whatever was planned for us near that forest in the morning.

The kind Slovak locomotive engineer risked his life to save approximately 200 Ukrainian refugees from groundless execution by the communists. This was on 2 November 1944.

Being so close to execution three times (and in three different places, by three different political regimes or groups: Nazis, communist partisans, and Soviet communists) did not bother me at the time. It seemed normal. I was 8 and 9 years old then. Nevertheless, memories of those events must have remained dormant in my mind, waiting to be triggered at some unrelated moment. About 30 years later, in April 1973, I was about to hold an oral defense of my doctoral dissertation at the University of Pennsylvania. The night before, I had a dream.

Everything was in shades of grey, with no vivid colors, except for a narrow stream of light landing on the brick wall behind me. I was 9 years old in this dream. For some reason, I stood in a prison courtyard, facing a firing squad made up of men in varied uniforms. Some had dark Nazi uniforms, others Soviet ones, or just a mix of the work clothes of communist partisans or other police. They all stood in one line.

They represented a firing squad. And they were all looking at me. Then, they raised their rifles, all of them pointing at me. What WAS I to do?!

I shut my eyes and tried to find a way out of this situation. I thought that I shouldn't be standing, only moving. Where to? There was a wall behind me, and in front of me were rifles aiming at me. Quickly, find another direction! I forced myself to become smaller and smaller (a sort of "Alice maneuver"). Then, just as the order to fire was shouted (I can't remember in what language it was given!), I managed to turn into a m o u s e and disappear into a hole. Then I heard the shots.

And my dream ended.

The next morning, rather shaken, I took a train from Princeton, New Jersey to Philadelphia and nervously walked the five blocks to the university. Along the way, I happened to meet Dr. Murl Barker, my professor of Symbolist Poetry, who was on my dissertation committee. Prof. Barker noted that I was a little tense, and asked me what happened. I related my dream to him. He was very empathetic, and tried hard to convince me that the dream was actually "a good sign", or even a "positive symbol."

We walked to the room where the defense was scheduled to take place; the place was reasonably well lit, with a stream of sunlight coming from the window behind the head table. Prof. Barker accompanied me to the table, pulled out a chair, and asked me to take a seat. I took one step towards it, when suddenly he turned white and blocked my way to the chair. Then he dropped a newspaper on it and gently steered me towards another chair, claiming that the first one was covered by a lot of dust and chalk. But before he dropped the newspaper, I managed to see what caused his distress: on the chair, where I was to sit, was a dead, white m o u s e !

No wonder that my professor of Symbolist Poetry reacted that way! The other professors who were on my dissertation committee were not aware of my dream, nor of the dead creature on the chair, nor why I was switching chairs. They just smiled supportively.

After my successful defense, I was concerned about the physical aspect of that "symbolic sign" on the chair, and decided to take a peek at the mouse again. How shocked I was when the mouse was not under the newspaper anymore!
It too had played dead and then disappeared!
It too managed to outmaneuver its own possible execution, just as I outmaneuvered both the oneiric one, and the threats of the real ones, many years ago...

Chapter 12

THE STRASSHOF NAZI TRANSIT INTERNMENT CAMP

When the train from Bratislava (Slovakia) arrived in Vienna, on 2 November 1944, and then Strasshof, many young people took care to disappear quickly with their belongings. They either knew where they could get help, or relied on their youth and strength to manage on their own. But most of the families with young children, after being dropped off from the train, just remained about a dozen yards from the railroad tracks. It was an area where city people had their little vegetable plots and huts. We stayed there for a day, until the Nazi authorities herded us to the Strasshof Transit Holding Camp.

For thousands of refugees from Central and Eastern Europe, this was the first step to Nazi camps. It was here that people from a dozen nationalities were disinfected and sorted, and then sent to their various fates (labor brigades, labor camps, concentration camps, and factories). This was a transit camp for refugees and foreigners, or the "non-Aryan" *Untermenschen* [German for "subhuman" or inferior men]. In contrast, the German people considered themselves to be a "master race" of "Nordic" Europeans.

That first part of being "sorted" and registered in that camp remains very clear in my memory. We were grouped by gender and sent to different parts of the building. In the women's section, we had to undress completely and submit our clothing for disinfection, while we all showered together in the open. And what a shock it was to see hundreds of women of all ages completely naked. It was a most undignified sight; although many women were old, sick, or injured, they were not allowed to keep even their bandages. My young friends and I worried whether the bones of the extremely fragile people would break first, or would pierce through the skin and be scattered. Some of the women had very large and flabby tummies; my slightly older girlfriends, "expertly" explained that this happens when a woman bears at least 10 children. Surprisingly, during this showering procedure, there were no voices of protest from the adults, as if the nakedness made them all quite meek.

After showering, we were given small, dark blue pieces of cloth. It was hard to decide what part of my naked body to cover; however, since I was only 9 years old then, I was not as concerned about the top part being exposed. But I remember the struggle that tall young women had when they tried to stretch that blue cloth to cover both the chest and the stomach areas. Some tried covering only the front – it worked, but left the backside exposed. All of these efforts by naked females were observed by groups of laughing young male soldiers, or guards in uniforms, with rifles in hand. Each refugee had to pass through a "medical inspection" – again, male "staff" checked semi-naked women and young girls! After we were reunited with our male family members and friends, we heard that the same thing happened in their quarters, except that they were given an even smaller piece of cloth, and the naked males were inspected by young female guards and checked by young female "medical staff."

The memory of that blue piece of cloth somehow remained buried in my subconscious. Fifty years later, before a medical procedure at a hospital, I had to have photographs taken of my body, and I was given a tiny, dark-blue triangle to cover my private parts. Unexpectedly, this brought back memories of the Nazi Strasshof camp, and it really perturbed me. It also brought to mind comparisons of concentration camps of the worst order, making me grateful that we experienced only the Strasshof camp.

Following the showering procedure, we were fumigated with some very strong chemical powder. My mother lost her underarm hair then, and it never grew back (at least that was some consolation!). We were then sent to barracks, each of which housed about 40 people. There were double- and triple-level metal bunk beds there. On one of them, my parents and I had the first two levels, while on the next bunk bed, a newly married Polish couple shared the second level. They were the talk and concern of the whole barrack. The man was a physics and math professor at a large Polish university (either Warsaw or Krakow University). Apparently, a day before the couple was to be married, some Poles had somehow angered the Nazis, who then announced that, in retribution, a certain quota of Poles had to be arrested the following day.

The Nazis used group punishment or summary executions to teach by example. Thus, if the local Ukrainian or Polish citizens stood up to the Nazis in some way, and especially if they killed a German soldier, a specific quota was placed on the "guilty" nationality. And then, they announced the number of Ukrainians or Poles that would be arrested and shot, or hanged, on a given day. The easiest way for the Nazis to fill a quota quickly was to go to a large gathering of people and immediately round up the given number of victims. And so they did on that particular day. As the marriage ceremony ended and the newlyweds and guests were leaving the church, they were all arrested, put onto a freight train, and sent off to Strasshof – while still wearing their wedding attire.

It was a surreal sight, worthy of a Bergman film: in a wooden barrack with dozens and dozens of people in shabby clothing, there was the bride in her long, satin gown (formerly white, now dirty, crumpled, and slightly torn), and wearing dainty slippers, while the groom wore a coat with tails. Everybody felt so sorry for them that the Ukrainian women refugees somehow managed to collect non-matching pieces of clothing that they gave the bride, so that she could at least change from her wedding gown. It was a very touching moment; certainly none of those in our barrack had clothing to spare, and yet they acted with such kindness.

While the bride and groom were assigned to our part of the barrack, fortunately, a young female guard directed the rest of the wedding party to another barrack. I thought, that this must have spared the newlyweds some feelings of discomfort from having to see their guests suffer in the camp every day – just because they had come to the couple's wedding.

Chapter 13

TRAINS AND BOMBS FOREVER?

After we and our belongings were well disinfected, and then we passed a medical screening at the Strasshof camp, my parents were ordered to do some menial jobs, while my pre-teen friends and I helped them by carrying bricks. After a few days, we were put on a freight train again, this time to Dresden. In the early hours of 7 November, we saw flyers dropped from a plane, informing us that Archbishop Andrei Sheptytsky died on the first of November. All the Ukrainians in the wagon felt as if they had suddenly been orphaned.

Several days later, off we were sent to Leipzig, where we had to undergo disinfection again. We were housed in a school. There wasn't much food, so my parents had to sell some pieces of clothing in order to buy bread and apples. Our next destination was a camp in Magdeburg. After one week there, off we went via Frankfurt to Pössen. I have no idea today (nor did my parents) why we were moved from one camp to another, but perhaps that was a blessing. There were worse possibilities.

Our path took us through Dresden and Leipzig. Dresden was being extensively bombed when we reached it. I remember an air raid there. We had to leave the train very quickly and lie down about 8 feet away from the railroad tracks. It was rather late at night and pitch black; suddenly, the sky was decorated by bursts of large orange-red "fireworks." We could hear the bombs swishing through the air and then exploding not too far from us. Hypnotized by the sight and the sound of the bombs, I just kept staring at the lights that kept appearing.

The fires caused by these bombs riveted me in place, instead of making me run away. Lying on the slope of the railroad tracks, I seemed to freeze up, turning into a static onlooker. It took a lot of self-discipline, or presence of mind, to grasp the reality and run, as my parents directed me to do.

Later, when we continued on to Leipzig, there were more air raid alarms and more bombings. One night, we managed to stay at a school where other refugees were sheltered. Next, as we traveled through Frankfurt to Pössen, one of our suitcases went missing! Our luggage (which was our "reality") also represented our only means of survival on various trains, in camps, farms, and cities. So when an item was lost, it meant more than just aggravation, or even the inconvenience of losing a needed item. There were several close calls, and a couple more actual losses, followed by unexpected twists of fate.

While we thus "visited" several camps and several cities, we also saw groups of local farmers regularly coming and looking for workers, since most of their men were at the front. Germany was short of workers then and was eager to find anyone willing to work. In the meantime, Father was able to contact the Duwalo family, our friends and neighbors from our hometown. They managed to get work in an Austrian town called Gattendorf, on a farm owned by Herr Peschke. Mr. Duwalo said he would ask the farmer about getting a sponsorship for us. Apparently Herr Peschke was very happy with Mr. Duwalo's work, and when asked to help our family, he gladly sent a request to the camp officials, asking them to allow us to come and work for him. Mr. Vasyl Duwalo had a degree in agronomy, knew much about farming (at least the theory of it) and was, therefore, quite useful on that farm. However, my father, a professor of Latin, and my mother, a teacher, had no experience in farming. So Herr Peschke really took a chance on us; quite likely, he just wanted to do a good turn for his friend. Although Mr. Duwalo cautioned Herr Peschke of what he was getting into, nevertheless the man agreed to help a family in need.

Germany was in need of workers! Thus on the basis of Herr Peschke's request, we were issued a work permit, as well as food and travel documents. With these papers in hand, we were able to leave the camp and the freight trains, and travel by ourselves, or even purchase food. But because of wartime irregularities in the administration of railroads, as well as the availability of trains, it took us quite some time to reach Herr Peschke and his farm in Gattendorf. We had to report to the local police in each city where we got off the train, and had to provide the papers from our sponsor. Although we were not traveling in freight cars this time, since we were armed with documents indicating that my parents had working papers, we still had to show our permit to ride in trains.

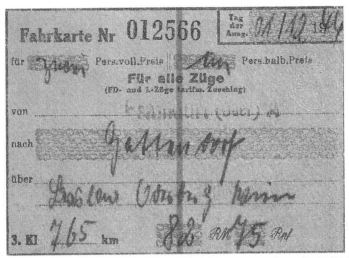

Photo 39-13. Our ticket, issued on December 1, 1944, for 2 adults (full fare) and a child (at half fare), cost 82.75 Reich Marks was for travelling 765 kilometers, from Frankfurt to Gattendorf

As we set off to Herr Peschke's farm, we had to take a train to Semmering, Vienna's suburban station. We spent the night at the train station before we were finally able to find a seat on the train. It wasn't an easy job, since we had all our belongings with us, and could not always manage to carry them all at the same time, especially on snow-covered and icy streets. Each one of us had several different pieces of luggage/bags to take care of. The city had been bombed just a day or two earlier, so there were many people seeking shelter at the station. Sitting there after midnight, we were hungry and tired. We huddled together on a bench, resting our heads on our knapsacks. My feet were swollen, so I took off my shoes, placed them inside the knapsack, and put on a pair of slippers.

In the middle of the night, something awakened me. Before I fell asleep, I saw that there were people sitting nearby, and now someone had just gotten up and left. Quickly, I inspected my knapsack! On one side there was a large cut in the shape of a capital "L"; it was big enough to pull a shoe out from the knapsack. *Yes, one shoe was missing!*

Quickly I checked inside the knapsack, where I had a spare pair of shoes. Yes, there was still one shoe on one side, and another shoe on the other side of the knapsack (we thought that packing shoes separately on each side would dissuade a thief, who would find only one shoe). Oh, good! I found one on each side and took them both out, planning to put them on. But what a shock awaited me: *both shoes were for the right foot!* What was I to do now? It was winter! How could I go anywhere without shoes?

My problem was solved in the following way: Mother went around asking people sitting at the station whether anyone could sell or trade a pair of boy's galoshes, which I could then put on top of my slippers. Unbelievably, she was successful, trading my father's leather wallet for galoshes. Now I could go outside, even in the snow!

After an alarm signaled the end of another bombing, off we moved again. We had to change trains, but finally reached our destination, although it was well after midnight. Mr. Peschke sent Mr. Duwalo and a horse-drawn wagon for us. We loaded our belongings on it and followed it on foot through a muddy forest. I remember that we placed my knapsack at the very top. When we arrived at the farm, we were eager to get some food and go to sleep, leaving our luggage on that wagon, which was stored in a barn.

In the morning, we went to get our belongings, and lo and behold – my poor, cut-up knapsack was not there. Someone was sent out to look for it along the road that we had taken. They even went all the way back to the station, but to no avail.

After staying for over a week at the farm, Mother was able to track down her sister and brother, who were staying in a small ski town called Semmering, about 25 km east of Vienna. My

Anmeldung
bei der polizeilichen Meldebehörde

7. Dez. 1944

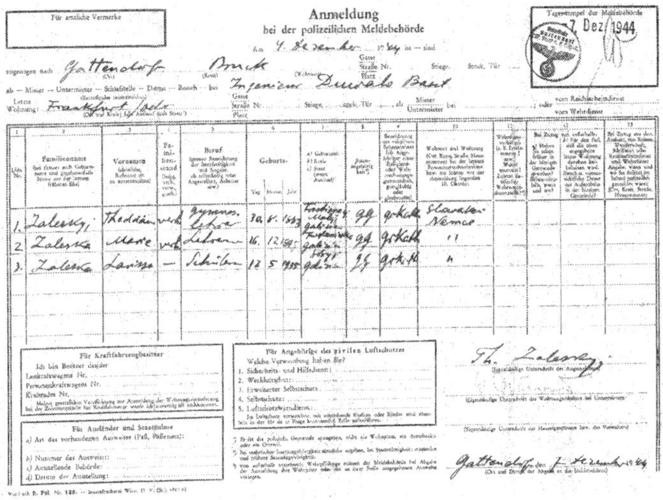

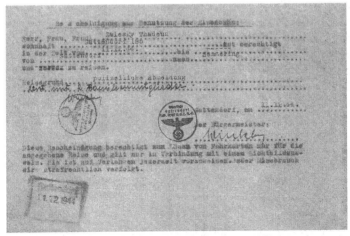

Photo 40-13. Police registration form. When we arrived, Father registered us at the police station, indicating where we were staying (with Mr. Duwalo, c/o Herr Peschke), and the road we needed to take to get to Gattendorf.

parents were well aware that we were of no help on the farm, so it was best to join Mother's siblings. We decided to thank Herr Peschke for his extreme kindness (for taking a risk in hiring us!) and asked him to release us from our promise to work for him. He agreed graciously, so off we went, taking various trains again.

Zalesky Thadeus

polizeiliche Abmeldung

Photo 41-13. Permission to take the train to Semmering

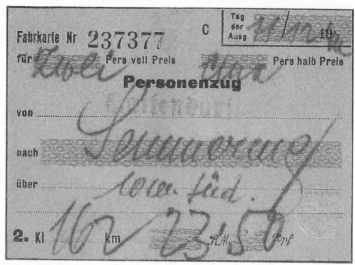

Photo 42-13. *Our ticket stated that we had paid for two adults and a child, a total of 23.50 Reich Marks, to travel 162 kilometers to Semmering*

And once again, we had to go through Vienna. It was 12 December 1944.The city has been heavily bombed, so there was no place to spend the night. But we knew that our family's close friend and dentist, Dr. Halyna Skoretska, had been assigned to work in Vienna (the Nazis did not allow her to practice in Ukraine, because she was suspected of treating insurgents). Father knew the city well, since he had lived there as a graduate student and lecturer immediately after World War I. So while Mother and I remained with our belongings under a tree, on a bombed street, Father went to look for Dr. Skoretska's apartment. After about an hour, he came back very discouraged, because that part of the city had been so badly damaged that he could not recognize the area at all (and after all, a quarter of a century had passed!), nor could he even tell where the various streets once were. There were no street signs, and almost no buildings remained intact in that area. What should we do? It was a gloomy and dark day, in every way. Mother could not go alone, since she did not know the city and did not know what street and building to look for.

On my suggestion, both my parents went together in search of their friend's building. I was left in charge of guarding our belongings. After about 20 minutes, there was an air raid alarm.

People were running to bomb shelters below ground. They were shouting to me to go and hide. But how could I? First of all, how would my parents know where I went? And secondly, I wouldn't be able to carry all the pieces of our baggage, so how could I leave the few worldly possessions that we still had?

Several streets away, planes were dropping bombs. I huddled, hiding under our knapsacks. It was a memorable experience. I was nine years old. Bombs were falling nearby. There was no time to look around – while I had to deal with the situation by myself. I was in a strange city, and I was alone. As I leaned on a tree between the sidewalk and the street, I kept thinking, what if something happened to my parents? What if the bombs hit them? What if the bombs hit me? What should I do?! I kept pressing my fingers against the bark of the tree, and finally hugged it. This contact with a concrete physical reality seemed to calm me. I continued to guard our luggage and waited for my parents, who soon ran back to be with me, and then together we went to the bomb shelter, dragging our belongings with us. During this particular experience, unlike during the previous bomb raids, I definitely *did not admire* the fiery sky, or the hypnotizing effects of the bombings. And I remember that in this unique predicament, I had to make an important decision all by myself, like an adult.

Chapter 14

MY KINGDOM FOR A HAIRPIN OR A
LEFT SHOE!

Traveling from city to city, occasionally going almost in a circle, everything felt unreal. Air raid alarms and bombs added to that feeling. But our belongings – that is, our knapsacks, bags, and suitcases – were ties to a reality that we had lost. They were a connection to our past and reminders that we once had a home and a country, and that once we even had a normal life – before the two uninvited invading powers showed up, one after the other, forcing their unwanted and cruel regimes upon us.

Now, our new reality was in the shape of a permit to travel to a ski resort town, called Semmering, not too far from Vienna. Yes, we were in Vienna again. It seemed that this city was destined to challenge us in many ways. The railroad station brought back memories of my experience there, when I had to wait for my parents and guard our luggage during an air raid. During these bombings, even children seemed to develop new skills. Such know-how included the ability to distinguish incoming planes by the sound that they were making. The most knowledgeable could tell whether it was a bomb carrier, and whether it had one engine or more. This knowledge certainly helped in deciding when to run and hide.

When I lost my poor, doomed knapsack on the way to the farm, besides my shoes, obviously, I also missed my clothing. But

91

most of all, I missed my *very first passport* with my photograph in it. It was proof of my existence and my identity. With losing my knapsack, I also lost all kinds of small items so necessary to a girl: my hairpins, for example. I was too old to keep my hair tied with a bow, and besides, I did not have any ribbons. My hair kept falling into my eyes, so we decided to try to buy a hairpin or two. While Father was waiting for us at the train station, Mother and I went looking for the rare store that was still intact and was open. After we finally found one, we went inside and asked, in German, for a hairpin. The storeowner found one, was ready to sell it to us, and then asked for an identification or ration card. After realizing that we were refugees, she barked that a hairpin was such a rarity that there were not enough even for Germans, let alone some foreigners! So, I had to continue putting up with my hair falling into my eyes.

Then off we went to rejoin Father. It was a cold day. There was a lot of snow and ice on the street, and we had to be very careful how and where to step. When we finally reached the station and managed to find a bench to sit on in the waiting room, we noticed that a very important item was missing: Mother's muff. In those days, in the wintertime, ladies carried large muffs not only to keep their hands warm inside them, but also to hold other items that would usually be kept in a purse. Actually, women thought that wallets and documents were safer in a muff, since both hands could touch and even hold them simultaneously. In her muff, Mother had our passports, our ration cards, and all our money. Since Mother also had other errands to take care of, so for awhile, she handed the muff to me. When we made a quick stop (to adjust the knapsack, so it would sit on the back more comfortably), suddenly we realized that I did not have Mother's muff anymore! Oh, how blood curdling was the panic! We were left only with the train tickets and travelling permit that Father held. At least we had those!

Mother quickly went to the local police station and reported the missing item, provided our forwarding address, and then we took the train to Semmering. We had to be very careful to have the necessary papers with us all the time. We did not want to be identified as "illegals" or some type of spies (that would have been the end of us!). At all our stops in Germany and Austria, not only were we required to register with the police, but as soon as we arrived, we also had to provide the name of a legal resident and an address where we were heading. This not only tracked us, but also allowed our mail to be delivered to that address.

During the war in Germany, buying any item for every-day use was a challenge for a refugee, and purchasing food wasn't any easier. We needed ration-cards for coal, as well as for food. Ration cards were good only for a specified period.

Photo 43-14. A ration card for vegetables and fruit

Finally, we could purchase some fruit! However, there was another hardship that we had to face; a rather daring and hazardous experience was awaiting us in this ski town of Semmering. We were staying with Aunt Sofia and her family (Uncle Oles, their daughter Chrystia, and Aunt's assistant Rozalia), as well as Uncle Lonhyn. We all lived in a tiny, three-room building, heated by a wood stove. It was a very cold winter and my parents had to go to the township office to ask for firewood. They were shocked to hear that neither firewood nor coal was available there, or anywhere else. But the official gave them a very practical (and kind!) advice. He said that during that particular winter, nobody had the luxury of going skiing for pleasure. The ski structures were not being used, and were starting to fall apart anyway, so he suggested: "Instead of freezing, why don't you cut down a few wooden planks from time to time, heat your place and save your lives? And forget that you heard this suggestion from me!"

Uncle Lonhyn volunteered for this nasty job, and drafted me to accompany him. It was a very terrifying and deeply embarrassing feeling: walking cautiously in the dark of night, and trying to break off one plank at a time with an axe. Every touch of the blade produced a loud echo, and the ski structure seemed to cry, whimper, and shake as if protesting (as was my mind and heart!). The whole experience felt so horrible, like a sin! I don't think that my parents would have ever stooped to allow me to participate in this undertaking, had it not been at the suggestion of that town official. I suppose he must have had an inkling which way the war was going, and felt that in the chaos, why not help several fellow human beings.

After we had spent four or five days in that town, Mother received a letter to come to Vienna. When she reported to the police station there, on 1 January 1945, she identified her missing muff! Someone had found it and returned it – with all the items intact! And during a war! Amidst the alarms and bombings, amidst the hundreds of displaced and needy persons milling around the city, someone had taken the time and effort to bring a lost item to the police station!

Somehow, we managed to deal with the cold and the snow. On 7 January 1945, we found a Roman Catholic church in town, and were happy to be able to hear Mass celebrated there. It was our Christmas Day. Eastern Christians celebrate Christmas on the 7th of January.

Chapter 15

A SCHOOLING ATTEMPT AND THE END OF WWII

In early February 1945, we packed our bags and headed to the province of Thuringia. It took us two days to reach Vienna, and then five more days to reach our friends in Pössneck, where the Boyanivsky family was able to find jobs for our adult family members. My parents and I, Uncle Lonhyn, Aunt Sofia, her husband Oles, my three-year old cousin Chrystia and Rozalia Shyian, were lucky to be allowed to stay in a signalman's station, which was actually just a little hut, though it felt like a large box. It was located between three railway lines, diverging from the main line immediately at the train station.

Since there was an increasing housing shortage caused by bomb damage, we were happy to get this hut, even though we were literally squeezed like sardines in there. That hut was supposed to serve one person, while there were eight of us! Inside there was no kitchen to speak of, only a small range, big enough to boil water in a kettle. An outhouse served as the "facility." The train rails were only about 6 feet away from both sides of our hut, so, no wonder it shook around the clock, from the loud rumblings of each train!

It seemed that all the trains had to pass our signalman's hut in order to load up at the heaps of coal. But those heaps of coal were also our lifeline: twice a week, we were allowed to fill up three pails of coal for our own heating and cooking purposes. We did this with team spirit: I would climb the heap of coal all the way to the top, and my two uncles would hand me an empty pail. I would then fill it up with smooth and shiny (almost like mirrors) bricks of coal, and lower them to the outstretched arms of my two uncles. They would then pick me up and lower me to the ground.

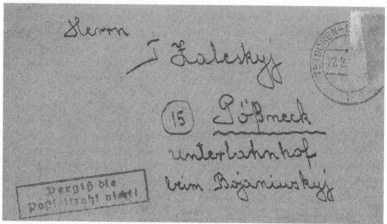

Photo 44-15. Our address, on the wrong side and between the tracks
Since our hut between the tracks did not have its own address
(and thus, no individual mail delivery), letters had to be directed to the
station, in care of a specific employee there

With the bombing continuing, we still had to report regularly to the police. All of our three adult males worked shoveling coal, feeding the train engines, carrying pieces of railing, and digging trenches. It was hard labor, to which my father (a teacher who was then 62 years old) and my uncles (a surgeon and an electrical engineer) were not accustomed. I suppose it was slightly easier for Father when he had to sweep streets or the main railroad station. Mother, Aunt Sofia, and Rozalia did some menial jobs. Although obviously everyone was physically exhausted by the end of each day, the important aspect of why we came to that town was that, with the jobs, we were also given food ration cards. That meant survival!

Our survival also included going to church. Although obviously there were no Eastern Catholic (Greco-Catholic) churches in Germany, we would go to any Christian church. We needed to. There were times when we experienced bomb alarms during Mass, and then everybody had to run to a bunker. Occasionally, a Ukrainian priest from another town would come to serve Mass just for us; I remember Rev. Bohdan Smyk, who came with his daughter Tania. Many years later, I met them again, but in the U.S.

It was not only on such occasions as Easter or Christmas that we went to church. I don't really remember where and how we managed to hear Mass in different cities, but whether it was a field Mass that a Ukrainian Greco-Catholic priest served, or an Orthodox Ukrainian Mass, or Slovak, Lithuanian, Polish, or German Roman Catholic – somehow we found an opportunity to hear one on many a Sunday. Father kept very elliptical notes on what we did each day, and left such notations as "went to Mass." If not to attend Mass, we often stopped just to see the inside of a church of any denomination, to find a couple of peaceful moments, or to calm the soul for a short while, and to say a prayer of thanks.

Going to hear Mass during war was not just comforting, but also made us feel part of humanity. It provided us with a touch of normal life that we no longer had, while we could still observe others in their routine. It also made us feel on par with others, forgetting the *Untermensch* brand.

Not too far from us was the town of Kahl, where Father and Uncle Lonhyn had to go on business one day. Upon their way back, they visited a castle there, where the daughter (or grand-daughter) of Kyiv's Prince Yaroslav the Wise (978-1054) lived for a time. The castle's employee who provided this information, was not certain about the name of that princess. Still, even to hear about this claim, was a pleasant surprise to us, almost like touching old Ukraine. We all knew about Yaroslav's daughter Anna, who became the Queen of France, but somehow, the fates of her sisters were not mentioned as much in history books (although two of her sisters also became queens of other European countries). I kept wondering how sad the princess must have been, being forced to marry a stranger from another country, and then having to move there, too. The price that princesses had to pay in order to keep peace in Europe! If only this could be done today, to keep wars away!

While the adults in my extended family were busy all the time with work, they were all concerned about any opportunity for my education, or rather the lack of it. After all, at that point of our journey, I had not attended school for a whole year. The only exotic educational "program" I had, was during an unplanned stop in Würzburg, where we were stranded for a couple of days. Father took me on an excursion; from the house (or actually the garage) where we were staying, we had to cross a bridge to the nearby forest. There, we walked a little distance before he introduced me to the legend of the Niebenlungen saga. It was in that forest that Siegfried (the hero of the story) was supposedly bathed in dragon's blood, and thus became invincible, except for one spot on the back of his neck, where a leaf fell from a tree during the bathing. Siegfried's whole body became invincible, except for the part under the leaf. Variants of the legend were popularized both in literature and in music.

Since we seemed to remain in Pössneck for a few more weeks, a family council was called to make plans for my homeschooling. As a result, I had individual teachers for the following: Ukrainian and Latin (Father), German, music, and drawing (Mother), hygiene/anatomy and astronomy (Uncle Lonhyn), and geometry (Uncle Oles). I think that Aunt Sofia was in charge of making certain that all these classes were held on time, and that I attended them!

All my teachers assigned lots of homework and insisted on checking it daily. But there was a problem with supplies: I had only one pencil, and there was no paper available to write on. Any possible scrap of used paper (including paper bags!) that had a blank spot on one side, had to serve as my notebook. Besides the lack of books and writing supplies, as well as the lack of sleep (because of the noise of the passing trains that we could almost touch from our hut), the daily pressure of expectations from my teachers was overwhelming me. I started to protest, saying that except for my parents, both my uncles and aunt were not professional teachers and should not be expected to serve as teachers (at least, I did not expect them to) if they could not provide me with any writing paper. They were my dearest family and my very good friends, but changing professions, even in wartime, did not appear to me to be the right thing to do. They had no textbooks, and I had no notebooks – so what kind of a school could this be?

All those adults and their expectations! I started a hunger strike, which lasted two days. Obviously, I had never heard of that word, or its concept. I just felt that the "pretend school" was very unfair to me, and it just wasn't a "serious approach to education" to lower the standards of schooling in this manner!

Then a new family council was called, which decided that I should attend a local German school with children my own age. My first two days were quite challenging there. This was the end of the last semester of the school year, and I had to fit into the program and the group of children. What bothered me the most was that this "regular" school also lacked books and writing supplies? Each child would bring a writing slate and chalk and take notes on it. We were also expected to do homework on the same slates. Although a slate looked like a mini blackboard (the size of a present day medium-sized computer tablet), it was very difficult to wipe off the hard, heavy, cheap chalk, the only kind that I could get.

I had to deal with two new tasks: to write in the German Gothic script and to somehow try to fit everything on the tablet. This was the hardest and biggest challenge! I could read texts written in Gothic, but writing was another matter. With my thick chalk, I could squeeze in only about 8 words on the 7"x12" slate, not more. But then there would be no room left for arithmetic! I did not want the German kids to look down on me, thinking that this foreign Ukrainian girl could not manage what they could! I kept wondering whether they had better chalk, or smaller fingers? After all, I hadn't touched a piano for over a year, so perhaps my fingers were getting stiff? I did not take into account that the German children had more experience with using the chalk over many months, or even years. They also had thinner sticks of much better quality chalk than I was able to acquire.

I struggled with that tablet for several days, and when I arrived in school one morning, I was saved from my suffering: *German soldiers have surrendered.*

Since the middle of April 1945, we saw white flags in the center of town, and then a few American flags. And then, on 4 May 1945, a group of American soldiers arrived in military vehicles, following a night of heavy aircraft rumblings and artillery shooting.

An unconditional surrender was signed by Germany on 7 May, to go into effect the following day.
We heard the official announcement on 8 May 1945:
GERMANY SURRENDERED!!!

O what a joyous day! What a happy day!
And happy Larissa! No more German school!
No more bombs!

The whole week was filled with high spirits and great hopes for the future, since on 6 May we celebrated Easter (Eastern Christian). We had a Lithuanian priest bless our traditional Easter baskets for us (with Ukrainian Easter eggs and Easter *babka*, but without the traditional butter, cheese, and sausage, since they were not available to us).

Easter Monday brought its own good news. According to my father's diary, a delegation from the Ukrainian group of workers in Pössneck went to the provincial center in Saalfeld, and was able to convince the people in charge of food ration cards to allow us 2,000 calories per day, rather than the 1,200 that our working members were getting. My whole family was most optimistic. Apparently, the highest calorie amounts were reserved for the Germans, then the French; next came Slavic people, and then Jews. At the same time, Uncle Lonhyn was told to report to work as a surgeon in a hospital for foreigners in the next town, Saalfeld.

Then, on that glorious 8 May, Ukrainian refugees in Pössneck also formed a committee to provide assistance/support to other Ukrainians, many of them in camps. Uncle Lonhyn was elected head, my father his deputy, Mr. Chalupa secretary, Mr. T. treasurer, and Mr. Mytka for liaison.

On 12 May, for my birthday, Father bought me a knapsack to replace the one that was lost at our previous location. Yes, obviously it meant that we were fated to be on the road again. We became nomads, although not by our own choice.

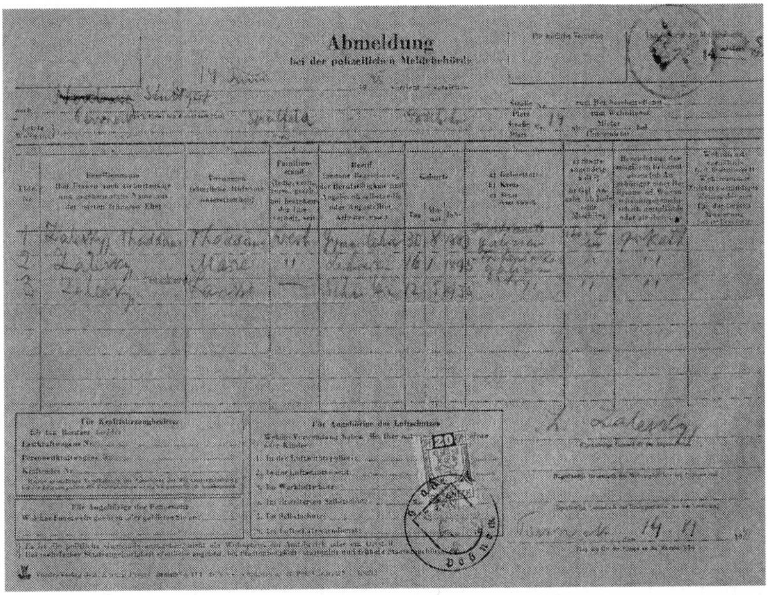

Photo 45-15. Police Registration form
*In order to leave town, we still had to get police permit and provide the
address of our destination.*

During the first days of May, we still had to register with the
local police, who used the same registration forms as during the
war. The form below has one main difference in one of the columns.
Question 8a asked from what state/country the registrant is (our
reply was "Stateless"). Question 8b asked whether one is Jewish
or of mixed race. The form was printed in Erfurt, Thuringia.
N.B., this question was not on a similar registration form of
11 December 1944 (i.e. still during the war) that we filled out
in Gattendorf. That registration form was printed in Vienna,
Austria. There is probably an explanation for this, whether one
local administration was more tolerant than the other, or perhaps
a much simpler reason.

Chapter 16

FORCED "REPATRIATION" TO – SIBERIA?!

The first months after the war were almost as stressful as those during it. Although bombs were not falling or exploding, it felt as if some kind of noose was tied around our necks, attempting to pull us towards a precipice. We survived the battle only to be pulled towards the hell of repatriation, which was not even to our own patria!

After the war there was no changing of the guard, only of enemies! When, in 1943, we witnessed the changing of totalitarian dictators, from the Russian to the Nazi, it was a repeat feeling of an entrapment; and then, one invader left, and another replaced him. And they were both alike. Was there really no end to their presence and their atrocities?

It was in February 1945, when the war was still going on, that a conference of the Allies was held in the city of Yalta. There, Stalin was able to convince his partners (Roosevelt and Churchill) that after the war, all "Soviet" citizens were to be repatriated, including people from the countries occupied only from 1939-1941 (Western Ukraine and the Baltics). It was because of the Yalta decisions that as soon as the war ended, Russian or Soviet representatives eagerly pursued thousands of refugees in order to put them on trucks and trains going *east*. And Western Allies did *not* protest.

Russian officials were joyfully riding in American jeeps, with red flags attached. They visited refugee groups and camps, saying that "their former citizens" *had to return* "*home.*" It was almost impossible to explain to Americans that we were *not* Soviet "citizens," and, definitely we were not Russians!

The Soviets had invaded the western part of Ukraine in 1939, and were there until 1941! That made us "Soviet?" In some camps, Russians even convinced Americans to list all Ukrainians simply as "Russians," so that the move would be simplified and automatic. Ukrainians protested. Many said that they would rather be shot on the spot. And some actually were shot, while others took their own lives rather than be taken to the Soviet Union. The repatriation fever was creating chaos and fear.

When the war ended, the victorious Allies divided Germany into military zones, as it was decided in the Potsdam Agreement (July 1945). There were to be the following zones: American, British, French, and Russian. Actually, the latter should have been called "Soviet," but everyone knew that Stalin and Russia made all decisions, so the "Russian" label stuck. The four zones were to be administered separately. My family was lucky to be in the American Zone of Germany. American representatives had to deal with and provide for tens of thousands of refugees and several million workers that the Nazi took by force to work for them.

At the end of the war, there were over 2 million Ukrainians in Germany and Austria; they were *Ostarbeiter*, prisoners of war, and refugees from the front line areas. Most Ukrainians in the Soviet/Russian Zone of Germany were the first to be forced to "repatriate" to the Soviet Union. No exact statistics is available regarding what percentage of the Ukrainian refugees the Soviets actually allowed to return to their hometowns and how many were sent straight to Soviet GULAGs.

Of the 200,000 Ukrainian refugees in West Germany, who refused to be repatriated, many were like my family, people from the western part of Ukraine, who were definitely not "Soviet citizens." I remember several periods of panic among Ukrainians from the eastern part of Ukraine, who actually could be called "Soviet citizens" (since they had been under Soviet dictatorship for over 20 years). However, they did not trust any promises from the

Soviet representatives about "going home", and they knew from experience that few would ever reach their homes. Thus many tried to pretend they were from the western parts of Ukraine. They would pick a family from a certain town and try to learn everything possible about important facets of life and people there. Any ties to the west of the Soviet Union were considered lifesaving.

These were extremely tense days for many refugees. It seemed that the American and British organizations set up to help us were naively trusting the Russians and handing over anyone whom the Soviets claimed as "theirs." Those who were kidnapped or agreed to return, the Soviets would often treat as "potential enemies or spies," or would force them to become informers. Any wonder that those with any experience with the Russian/Soviet regime would not trust them, ever?

There were countless delegations going to plead with the American representatives, but the latter believed that the Soviets would be fair and understanding. Whenever the Russian soldiers became aggressive, we informed them that American officials promised us, that the Soviets would *not* do anything unfair or untoward. To this, the Russian soldiers would only laugh: "Those gullible chocolate-eating soldiers claimed that?" I couldn't understand why the Russian soldiers were laughing at the American soldiers, and in particular, what was wrong with eating chocolates? After all, in the very distant past (i.e. my past!), I always had a very pleasant experience eating chocolate.

Father's diary noted the alarming news about Soviet soldiers kidnapping refugees for "repatriation" to the USSR. The refugees wanted to leave town, but as of 12May 1945, were not allowed to. As representatives of the Ukrainian group, Father and Uncle Lonhyn went to the town of Kahl, where there was a camp with three thousand Ukrainians whom the Soviets registered as "Russians." The Chief of the local police told the Ukrainian delegation, that "all Soviet citizens" would be "repatriated" the following day. On 19 May, Russian soldiers arrived, escorted by Americans, and under red flags. Dozens and dozens of trucks left with these Ukrainians, forced "to go home" to the USSR.

In Pössneck, there were 80 Ukrainians, but the Soviets somehow managed to provide a list of 120. The Ukrainians tried to explain why the refugees were refusing to have anything to do with the Soviets. A local German official complained that the refugees were using up ration cards, and thus not leaving much food for the Germans. He preferred to be rid of us.

In my father's mini journal for 20 May 1945, when we were in the town of Pössneck, he wrote about the suicide of a Ukrainian refugee, who preferred death rather than submit to forced "repatriation." There were many more such examples. Gen. Eisenhower finally grasped the unfairness of forcefully handing over unwilling people to the Russians, and in October 1945, banned forced repatriation. However, repatriation actions resumed the following year.

There were numerous similar incidents. On the 21 May 1945, local government officials informed us that refugees from 10 specific nationalities (Ukrainians, Bulgarians, Poles, Byelorussians, Romanians, Finns, the three Baltic nations, plus one which I don't remember) *would not be forced to return to their home countries.* This was to be the law while Thuringia was under American administration. But it was to change soon, when on 1 June 1945, the provinces of Saxony and Thuringia would become part of the Soviet Zone, as the Russians demanded.

This change threatened our stay in Thuringia. Immediately my extended family, together with four other ones, decided to leave Pössneck as soon as possible. We wanted to reach the area of Germany that was under American control. During our escape, we stopped to rest on the outskirts of a small town. Unexpectedly, someone came and warned us that Russians were in town and were grabbing refugees and loading them on trucks, to be forcibly taken to the Soviet Union. And here we were, with our luggage, and with no buildings nearby, only a small wooded area in which to hide.

Everybody had a different suggestion as to what to do. Aunt Sofia, as always, came up with a psychological approach to this very threatening situation: put all our belongings into one pile, and let a child sit on top, while everybody else hid in the woods. I agreed to act in this performance. The staging was to confuse the Russians. We were hoping to create the impression that we were from a distant German town, taking a break, on our back home after working in the area. So all the adults and the other children quickly ran into the woods.

The Russians arrived within minutes, and stared at this girl of 10 sitting on numerous pieces of luggage, holding a German book, hugging her doll, and staring back at the men. They asked me something in Russian (which I did not understand), and I kept replying in German, "I don't know..." ["*Ich weiss nicht*"]. The soldiers (who spoke no German), not knowing who and how many we were, became confused. They were also suspicious that there was something more to this situation than met the eye, that it could be a trap or something, so they gave up trying to get any information out of me and left us in peace. What an unbelievably lucky escape for all of us!

We got back on the small "Praha" brand truck, when we passed a town that had previously held a Nazi camp for *Ostarbeiter* (slave laborers) from Ukraine. We saw a commotion, and stopped by the gate. There were Russian soldiers in army trucks, grabbing young people to repatriate them to the "Glorious Homeland." Three young Ukrainian women ran through the gate, and when they heard us talking in Ukrainian, they pleaded with us to take them with us. There certainly was no room in the tiny "Praha," but Lubomyr Mudry (later Rev. Lubomyr), wished to save them. The three women (I remember the names of two of them: Stakha B. and Mushka B.) eagerly joined us and we quickly left town, hoping the Soviets would not pursue us. Another happy ending to another tense situation! The young women (about 19 years old) were doubly fortunate: their respective families left Ukraine in the hope of finding their daughters, and soon were actually able to unite with them! This was achieved through a very effective network of Ukrainian refugees exchanging information through their committees.

A year later, another incident with the communists had a dire ending. My Aunt Edi and her family were then in a Ukrainian DP camp in the town of Füssen. On 1 June 1946, Russian representatives came interviewing people and taking them by force. A day or two later, Soviet trucks came around again, and Soviet soldiers were ordering people to get on the trucks and return to "the Fatherland." Obviously, no one volunteered. But the Soviet representatives had lists of camp residents and information about their places of birth, and started threatening people with punishment for their families in the home country. When my Aunt heard the threats, she had a stroke and died within hours, leaving my two cousins Lida and Chrystia Zaleska, aged 8 and 16 respectively, with only their elderly grandmother.

Photo 46-16. Aunt Edita Zaleska's funeral

It was always very painful for the refugees to experience funerals of one of their own, because somehow it emphasized their temporary presence in the given area, and elevated the fear that they were leaving their loved one in a strange country, without much hope for visiting that grave again. It was doubly painful this time, since the reason for my Aunt's death left many people quite shaken.

As a result of the Allies' blind support of USSR's demands of repatriation, close to 2 million people were forced to "go home." Those who refused to "return," Moscow labeled "war criminals," because it suggested failure of the communist system to keep them obedient.

The need for international protection of refugees from forced repatriation may be demonstrated by Eleanor Roosevelt's extensive and continued efforts to bring change through the United Nations, which finally passed the Universal Declaration of Human Rights in 1948. However, it was only in 1951 that refugees were to be protected from being forced to return (The Geneva Convention on Refugees). Unfortunately, it was too late for the thousands and thousands who were already in various GULAGs.

Chapter 17

SEARCHING FOR SAFETY IN GROUPS: THE AUGSBURG CAMP

By June 1945, my family and our Ukrainian co-refugees realized that we would probably be rounded up and repatriated if we stayed by ourselves, and that we should seek security amidst a larger Ukrainian group. We were especially vulnerable as "stateless" refugees. Because Ukraine was not independent then, "stateless" people were treated according to the interpretation or whim of any official.

Out of over 16 million foreigners in Austria and Germany, two million were Ukrainians, most of whom had been taken to Germany for slave labor. They were primarily young people (about a third of them were taken as young as 12 or 14) who had not completed their secondary education yet. Many were also held in Nazi concentration camps and in prisoner-of-war camps, and were now rescued.

By the end of 1945, all refugees who were in East Germany, as well as many in West Germany, were repatriated to the Soviet Union. The 200,000 Ukrainians, who were left in West Germany, resisted deportation by all possible means. Many renounced their former citizenship. Since Ukraine was not independent at the time, the citizenship was not Ukrainian anyway, but that of the country that occupied their part of Ukraine at the time: Poland, or Czechoslovakia, or the USSR. Thus, many Ukrainians were classified either as citizens of the above countries, or were simply classified as "stateless."

Since so many Eastern European refugees refused to return to Russian/Soviet or communist occupied areas, the Allies organized temporary camps for the refugees, who were then called "Displaced Persons" (or "DP's"). They were not so much "displaced" as just unwilling to be "placed" back in their country of origin, which was at the present time under Russian rule.

Although Europe was in a state of chaos, the world of the "DPs" was intensely busy with organizing their new (though, temporary!) settlements. Usually, the Allies settled the camps mostly by nationalities. Also, the Allies were pretty lenient in arranging for the refugees to stay in camps where they had relatives or friends.

At the end of August 1945, our extended family reached the city of Augsburg, and searched for a DP camp that would take us. After about a week, we received permission to stay at the Sommekaserne camp in that city. It was a different experience from our previous nomadic life. In the DP camp, there were more than a thousand people just like my family, and the camp worked like a small town. There were schools, a Scouting group, theatres, choirs, etc.

I was quite impressed with the fact that several very important people from Ukraine resided in the Augsburg Ukrainian DP camp, people with names that even I knew. Among them was Dr. Olha Kosach Kryvyniuk, an older sister of the leading Ukrainian poet, who wrote under the pen name Lesia Ukrayinka. Dr. Kryvyniuk was completing a detailed biography of her famous younger sister (Larysa Kosach Kvitka, 1871-1913).

Dr. Kryvyniuk was terminally ill at that point, but somehow a group of Scouts was allowed to visit her. It was an unexpected honor for me to be also included, and it felt as if, through the sister, I was almost meeting the poet Lesia Ukrayinka herself. In the Ukrainian culture of the day, poets were considered to be the most important public personas. I already knew some of Ukrayinka's poems, loved them greatly, and often recited them. This meeting was exceedingly important to me also because my father chose my own first name, Larysa/Larissa, in honor of Lesia

MILITARY GOVERNMENT OF GERMANY

TEMPORARY REGISTRATION   Zeitweilige Registrierungskarte

Name   **Z a l e s k a Marie**   Alter **49**   Geschlecht **weiblich**
Name   *Age*   *Sex*

Ständige Adresse   **Jaroslau / Polen**   Beruf **Lehrerin**
Permanent Address   *Occupation*

Jetzige Adresse   **Augsburg, Sommekaserne Langemärkstr.**
Present Address

Der Inhaber dieser Karte ist als Einwohner von der Stadt   **A u g s b u r g**
vorschriftsmäßig registriert und ist es ihm oder ihr strengstens verboten, sich von diesem Platz zu entfernen. Zuwiderhandlung dieser Maßnahme führt zu sofortigem Arrest. Der Inhaber dieses Scheines muß diesen Ausweis stets bei sich führen.

The holder of this card is duly registered as a resident of the town of **A u g s b u r g**
and is prohibited from leaving the place designated. Violation of this restriction will lead to immediate arrest. Registreant
will at all times have this paper on his person.

Kennkarte Nr. 11224

Legitimations-Nummer
Identity Card Number   Name and Rank
     Mil Gov Officer U.S. Army

Zaleska Marie   **3. 9. 45**

Unterschrift des Inhabers
Signature of Holder   Right Index Finger   Datum der Ausstellung
     Date of Issue

(Dies ist kein Personal-Ausweis und erlaubt keine Vorrechte.)
(This is not an identity document and allows no privileges.)

1. Waren Sie Mitglied der Nazi-Party zu irgendeiner Zeit, der SS oder SA? (Ja oder nein) **nein**

2. Waren Sie seit dem 1. Januar 1933 in der Wehrmacht, Marine, Luftwaffe, Waffen-SS? (Ja oder nein) **nein**

Familienstand   **verh.**   Staatsangehörigkeit **Staatenlos**

Welche Tätigkeit bisher gemacht?   **Lehrerin**

Waren oder sind Sie im Besitz eines Arbeitsbuches? (Ja oder nein)   **nein**

Jetzt beschäftigt?   **nein**   (wenn „ja"): Wo?

Wo zuletzt beschäftigt?   **Schule in Strys**

Fremde Sprachen: (1)   **deutsch poln.**   gut? (2) **gut**   gut?
     wenig?   wenig?

Geburtstag und Jahr   **18. 12. 1895**   Arbeitsfähigkeit **ja**

Familienangehörige unter 14   **1 Kind**

Name	männlich oder weiblich	Alter
Zaleska Larisa	**weiblich**	**1935**

Photo 47-17. Permit to stay in the Augsburg Sommekaserne camp
Note that my mother is listed as stateless ("Staatenlos"). The first
question asks whether the person was a Nazi Party member or served in
the SS (Defense Corp) or SA (Assault Division).

Ukrayinka. Seeing one of her three sisters was almost like being able to touch history. To this day, in my memory, I associate any mention of Augsburg with that meeting. A decade or so later, I spent many a day over the heavy volume of the biography that

Dr. Kryvyniuk wrote about her sister; in fact, for me (as well as for most other researchers of L. Ukrayinka), it became an unparalleled source book on the poet's life.

My first contact with Americans, seeing American soldiers on the street, brought a certain feeling of security. These men were neither the creepy Nazis nor the uncouth and unpredictable Russian soldiers. They were rather funny, chewing gum most of the time, and smoking. The end of the war meant a very limited availability of certain products, including cigarettes. In our family, only Uncle Oles smoked, and he certainly painfully felt the shortage of cigarettes. We often saw American soldiers smoking cigarettes and throwing them out half-smoked. It turned the stomachs of so many smokers, among them my uncle. Many men would quickly pick up the butts, but not Uncle Oles. It would have been quite an incongruous scene if he did: he was tall, slim,

Photo 48-17. On the left, an I.R.O. representative from Canada (Mr. Stodt); my cousin Chrystia, Uncle Oles, and Aunt Sofia Nehrebetsky

with a very distinguished face and bearing! I don't remember how things got to the point that I volunteered to pretend that I was kicking the butts for fun, and then would quickly pick them up and throw them into a paper bag. Uncle Oles would cut the butts open, take out the tobacco and roll a fresh cigarette. If there is a special smoker's heaven, he looked as if he had reached it then!

When we were staying in the DP camp, Uncle Oles' luck improved; he was drafted to work for UNRRA (United Nations Relief and Rehabilitation Administration) and IRO (International Relief Organization), because of his knowledge of French, English, German and 3 Slavic languages. With his new position came normal food rations for his family, and finally the luxury of having real cigarettes!

A few months later, adults in the DP camps were also provided with packs of cigarettes, which soon substituted for the German currency or Reichs Mark (RM). However, prices were becoming sky-high and black market was king. On 21 June 1948, there was a currency reform in West Germany, with 10 RM exchanged for 1 DM (Deutsche Mark); this stimulated normalization of product and food availability. Imagine paying in DM ten times less for a loaf of bread! It seemed to improve people's mood, even if it actually represented the same value as in RD x10!

Chapter 18

THE SHAPING OF A POSTWAR LIFE: THE NEU-ULM CAMP

After staying in Augsburg only several weeks, we moved to Reinhardt-Kaserne in Neu-Ulm, where Mother's siblings were already. Prior to WWII, the camp was built to serve Germany's soldiers, and now it housed refugees who were displaced by Germany's war. There were five large buildings, plus several garages for army trucks, and more. In each of these buildings, there were three floors plus an attic, where there were 8 large rooms, each housing 8-10 people. Also, each floor had an officer's apartment (including a private bathroom!) with two bedrooms. This was a luxury that very few were fortunate enough to enjoy. There were also several "single" bedrooms on each floor, which were now assigned to individual families.

We were among those who had a small separate room that held two single beds and a small desk. We also had a hot plate for cooking occasional small meals. There were shared bathrooms and group shower facilities at the end of each corridor, serving about 30 people.

Photo 49-18. Refugee children enjoying a birthday party in small, one-room residential quarters in the camp (1947). My cousin Chrystia Nehrebetska is the first one on the left.

The general mess hall offered us coffee in the morning, powdered pea soup for lunch, and tea and porridge for supper. For all of this we were most grateful. But there were situations when we could get a glimpse at more "normal" menus, even in hospitals. One time Mother was hospitalized in a German hospital in the old city of Ulm; hospitals were able to provide meals totaling 2,000 calories per day. When I came to visit Mother, she shared a buttered Kaiser roll with me. That was a treat! On another occasion, several students from our Gymnasium (*high school*) and I were taken to a hospital to have our tonsils and/or adenoids taken out. There we were given food and even ice cream, and this erased the unpleasantness of the surgery itself. With no anesthetics available, the patient had to sit on the lap of a very strong nurse (who held my feet with her own, while also holding my arms at my back), and thus the surgery proceeded. The process left two bloodstains on my pastel green dress (no hospital gowns were available)! It was not a pleasant experience, but since there was a group of us who underwent the same procedure, no one complained, especially when our thoughts turned to the Kaiser rolls and the piece of orange that we were promised.

In terms of clothing, from time to time, we received items donated by the good and kind people of Australia, Canada, and United States, through UNRRA (The United Nations Relief and Rehabilitation Administration). It was organized in 1945, and then in 1947 its work was taken over by a UN subsidiary, the International Relief Organization (IRO). In our camp, both these institutions were run primarily by officers from the US, Canada, Great Britain, and Australia.

Photo 50-18. Ukrainian Women's Organization in Neu-Ulm. It included women of all professions and from all regions of Ukraine. My mother is in the 2nd row, 2nd from the right. The uniformed ladies in the front row are from IRO: Miss Levy (in a jacket) from Canada, and Miss Valerie Paling (on the right) from Australia, the uniformed lady in the center (not identified is from the U.S.).

This 12-year old grew fast and soon had problems finding clothing to wear, particularly something suitable for special occasions. The IRO clothing was not always available in all sizes. Here my family was very helpful. Since I was now the same size as Mother and Aunt Sophia, as well as Rozalia, they allowed me to wear their dresses when there was need to look more presentable.

Photo 51-18. Mother and I, sporting clothing donated by UNRRA or IRO

Photo 52-18. Finally, we are the same height! Rozalia Shyian (Dulyba),
Aunt Sophia Nehrebetska, I (now able to fit into my Aunt's dresses),
and Mother.

Photo 53-18. The Reinhardt-Kaserne in Neu-Ulm provided a view of the famous Gothic cathedral in the "Old" Ulm. At 530 feet or 161 meters in height, it was considered the tallest church structure in the world, built between the fourteenth and nineteenth centuries.

The beautiful Ulm cathedral (although lacking a bishop) was the largest in Southern Germany, with great artwork and lovely architecture. The church had an organ on which Mozart had played. Throughout the war, the cathedral remained miraculously intact. Students from our Gymnasium, as well as countless other refugees, visited the structure, proud of making it all the way to the top after climbing 768 steps, in order to admire the view of the whole surrounding area.

The city itself was in pretty bad shape; many ruins of buildings that had been bombed were still not cleared away, and obviously would not be restored for several years yet. In my diary for 13 January 1948, I made a note stating that in the Old City (Ulm), a large cement block fell off a top of a building while one of our teachers was walking along the street below. The block hit two women: one was seriously injured, while the other one, Miss Vira Liubanska (our English language teacher in the Gymnasium), sustained a crushed leg and stomach. She died after being admitted to the hospital. We were all quite shaken by this.

In the Ukrainian DP camp in Neu-Ulm, there were people from all parts of Ukraine. My friends often shared descriptions and stories about their cities (e.g. Tania described Kyiv, Liolia told us about Vinnytsia, while Alla and Olia talked about Rivne and Lutsk). In terms of religious affiliation, camp residents were mostly Ukrainian Orthodox or Ukrainian Greco-Catholic. While I grew up mostly among Greco-Catholics, in my class there was almost an equal number of students of both faiths.

Since the chapels of both faiths were in the camp, I tried to get to know the Ukrainian Orthodox one. This was also the school's policy. According to my diary, on 22 January 1947, when Ukrainians celebrated the 1918 Independence Day, all the students attended a service at the Greco-Catholic chapel, and then for the liturgy we all went to the Ukrainian Orthodox chapel. This was a truly brotherly, ecumenical coexistence of Ukrainian students of the two faiths.

There must have been about two thousand people in our camp. I did not witness the organizing process, but the results were amazing! In a very short time, the camp acquired a distinctive infrastructure, that of a separate city: camp administration, police, medical department, education department (with kindergarten, primary and middle schools, high school equivalency preparation courses, as well as vocational training), theatre, and chapels (in what used to be army garages) for the two major Ukrainian religions. This was an educational experience for youngsters of both faiths, since Ukrainian Catholics (or Greco-Catholics) lived in the western parts of Ukraine, while the Orthodox predominated in the rest of the country, and did not often have an opportunity to meet.

The camp also had a soccer team, a newspaper, and book publishing. There were people of all professions and occupations, including professors, teachers, writers, musicians, actors, physicians, journalists, scientists, politicians, shopkeepers, farmers, laborers, and many others. Among the many personalities in the camp was our neighbor Ivan Bahrianyi, a very popular Ukrainian novelist, who also published a newspaper in the camp. Looking back at the photos now, I can see that in this camp, there were so many leading figures from Ukrainian cultural, academic, artistic, and intellectual life, as well as other fields, that together with those in other DP camps, they represented quite a *brain-drain for Ukraine*. On the other hand, had they remained under the Soviet regime, many of them would probably have rotted away in prisons or in Siberian GULAGs, since with each invasion,

Russians always made sure to annihilate Ukrainian intellectuals and community leaders first.

Although we did have textbooks, and there was a modest lending library, this did not satisfy all of us. I wanted to have my own books of my favorite poems and stories. So I started copying by hand some literary works that I liked, and compiled several such "anthologies." This labor of love stayed with me throughout my life, so, over the years, I published 6 anthologies, primarily of drama.

Photo 54-18. My very own personal anthology of my favorite poems, vol. II, 1947-1948

There was a common thread running through many of the poems that I collected. Often they were about finding a road to a lost home; or, they were allegorical poems about a tied-up giant who will wake up and break his bonds. Obviously, I also collected many love poems, satisfying the tastes of a teenager (or a young girl about to become one).

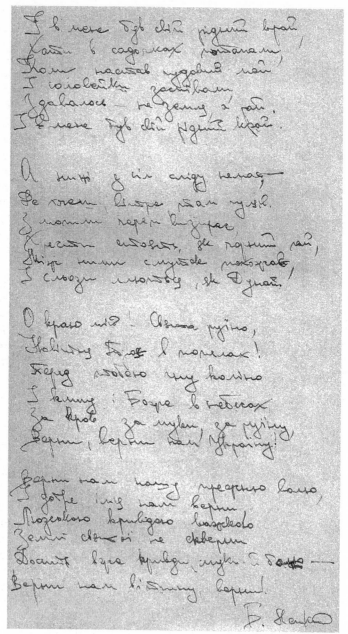

Photo 55-18. Part of a poem: "I, Too, Once Had a Country of My Own," by Bohdan Lepkyi. From my first anthology of poetry (vol. 1, 1946-1947, p. 72).

Since this was an early post-war situation, there were attempts to kidnap leading cultural figures in the camp in order to repatriate them to the Soviet Union. There were always stories about a spy appearing in the camp. There were also stories of assassinations. No wonder many people were so apprehensive every time Soviet soldiers appeared in town. Several of my girlfriends and I, considered ourselves "rather serious girls" (in contrast to the "silly girls"). We thought that we should train ourselves not to break in case of Soviet kidnapping and intense questioning (Nazis were no longer a threat to us after the war). Just in case we'd learn some important secret and be tortured for it, we'd have to be ready to withstand pain. So we got ourselves some cigarettes and matches and tried to hold lighted cigarettes against the skin on our arms. How long could we keep an important secret? We were able to increase our tolerance from two to five seconds. Then we decided not to continue and switched to memory games.

Otherwise, our activities provided some semblance of a normal life. Or perhaps a dream of what a "normal life" involves? Maybe it was because there were so many of us of the same age and in the same circumstances, and therefore this seemed like a "normal" way of life? Or because we realized that the war was over, so we felt truly happy. Perhaps our happiness was partly due to the fact that camp life was like living on an isolated island. It was almost like a ghetto, but a ghetto we entered by choice.

At the camp gate, there was always a guard checking who was leaving, and more importantly, what non-resident had a permit to enter the camp. We could leave the camp for longer or shorter periods of time, but we had to sign out. However, youngsters did not always feel like sticking to regulations. We found a way to climb the metal fence surrounding the camp and went sledding, for example. But our teachers were not happy with such mischief. Students who misbehaved in some manner, were usually punished by losing their right to leave camp for a week or two. While I was in the Second Form of Gymnasium (or Grade 7), my misdemeanor was reading a book that was allowed only in the Fifth Form (because of some allegedly inappropriate love scenes), and so I was not permitted to attend any theater performances in the camp, and was grounded in the camp for three weeks. In a way, I didn't mind; it gave me more time to read (or so I told myself).

But actually, we did not have much need to leave camp and deal with the German population. Personally, I didn't have much contact with them, except when I traveled by train to other cities, with others or by myself (from time to time, my Aunt would have me deliver something to Uncle Oles, who then worked in another city). Everything was so accessible in the camp itself, that we even went just across the street to pick flowers in the woods. I remember that my good friend Stefa V. was not only usually at the top of the class, but she was also the best flower picker of all of us – she had such nimble fingers! And of course, we went sightseeing Neu-Ulm as well as the old Ulm. We particularly loved the little island on the Danube that was actually part of the city of Old Ulm. And that was just about it, as far as daily contact with "the outside world."

Chapter 19

A PARADOXICAL BREATH OF NORMALCY FOR THE YOUNG IN CAMPS

Paradoxically, it was in a DP camp that my peers and I were able to experience the routine of a semi-normal life: I attended a Ukrainian school, saw Ukrainian theater performances and concerts, enjoyed the company of children my own age, and could finally become a Scout.

The feeling of normalcy was strengthened by the presence of a cat in our "residence." One morning, as I was putting my shoes on to go to school, I felt that my left shoe was filled with something warm. After investigating, I saw a little grey mouse run away. So all day long, I didn't dare put my foot into the left shoe. Was I forever doomed to have problems with my left shoe? When Mother related the story to a friend, the lady gave her a tiny kitten, called Uli. I gladly took Uli in, and from that time on, I had no unwanted residents in my shoes.

Our Gymnasium (High School)
The regularity of the school system had a very calming effect on the young. It seemed to run in a normal way. But who was I to judge what was "normal" in such circumstances? Compared to what? All my schooling took place during wartime. Although I never paid attention to brief adversities in life, I found a note in my Diary for 28 January 1947: "No school today; it was much too cold, and there was nothing to heat the building with." The 'building" in which the school was held, used to be an army garage,

with cement floors. It was subdivided by wooden partitions into classrooms, each of which held a wood or coal stove to heat it. Almost like American pioneer schools.

Our Gymnasium had Forms 1 through 8 (equivalent to Grades 6 to 12). Several teachers held doctorates and graduate degrees. Prof. Leonid Biletsky, a leading Kyiv literary scholar, was our principal and taught literature. Prof. Petro Tenianko taught history, Dmytro Nytchenko – Ukrainian language, Dr. Evhenia Kravchuk – geography, my father and Roman Dashkevych taught Latin, and Dr. Lonhyn Shankovsky– hygiene and science. The school was math-and science-oriented (rather than classics-oriented), but still included several foreign languages (Latin, German, and English) as compulsory. As soon as the schools were organized, it took only a short time to reprint pre-war Ukrainian textbooks in all the subjects and make many of them available to students.

Although Latin was taught from Form 2 and up (comparable to our Grade 7 and up), many students in the higher grades who had missed the first two years of Latin (as well as other subjects!) had to work hard to catch up. I remember my father always trying to make Latin accessible. When teaching the meaning of Latin words or grammar, he would often say, "It's just like in Ukrainian," especially in terms of declensions and cases. Both Latin and Ukrainian also have specific noun and adjectival endings for different genders; Latin has 7 cases, as does Ukrainian. The Ukrainian vocabulary also has a very significant portion of Latin derivatives.

We were grateful to our teachers for the work they managed to do in the circumstances, and considered the quality of teaching to be excellent. Students in our school were highly motivated, realizing that they needed to make up for at least two to four years of schooling that they missed during the war. Most of us managed it quite well. Looking at the photograph below, I recognize about twenty former students who later settled in North America. Three became mathematics professors, six college professors and scholars in other areas (including applied linguistics and theology), at least five became engineers, two teachers, while others include a pianist, an artist, a priest, a leading bilingual writer, a businessman, a banker, and several community activists. Many certainly relied on the education that they received from their teachers in the DP camp Gymnasium, in the unique camp setting.

Photo 56-19. The Neu-Ulm Ukrainian Camp Gymnasium students *(many in their scouts uniforms) and teachers (1947). Among them were: 3rd row from the left, 2nd - Miss Vira Liubanska, Larysa Zhyvaho, Tania Prushynska. From the right: 3rd - Mr Bedriy (geometry and drafting), Dr. Lonhyn Shankovsky (anatomy and hygiene), Mr. Roman Sohor (music). 4th row (sitting, from the left), 2nd- Mr. Balaban (science), Ms. X (German), Ukrainian Orthodox priest; Maj. Dolot (camp director), Dr. Leonid Biletsky (Ukrainian literature), Dr. Petro Tenianko (history), Dr. Evhenia Savchuk (geography), Prof. Tadey Zalesky (Ukrainian, Latin), and Mrs. Porokh (mathematics).*

There was one characteristic of some students that did not match typical high school demographics: many of those in the upper grades were two to four years older than the average student in the class. Usually they had no parents, nor family nearby. Many did not even know whether their parents survived the war. These were primarily the young people who were brought to Germany by force as slave laborers (*Ostarbeiter*). Now, they wanted to catch up in their education. They were given shelter in the DP camps, usually in large dormitory rooms. Dormitory life helped develop individual friendships and a certain sense of group belonging, as a replacement for the families that they did not have. They bonded and supported each other like a family, prodding each other to continue their education on college level. This bond was especially strong for those who came from the same city or village.

For adults who were in concentration camps, the numbers branded on their arms served as another bonding factor; they also formed their own association. Various organizations (especially the Association/Society of Ukrainian Women) in the camp tried to support the students without parents and help them in many ways. Not all of them adjusted well, and there was an attempted suicide.

The slightly older students still had a rather unique opportunity to be inspired in their educational process. Since living in the very close quarters in the camp was almost like sharing a house, not only was there an opportunity for daily personal exchanges with writers, artists, musicians, and educators, but also of finding role models or personal mentors. The presence of highly talented and respected individuals, together with the opportunity to attend performances, concerts, and talks several times a week, also must have made an impression on many students, especially in terms of encouraging their education.

The statistics for the 1945-1948 period, lists 110 Ukrainian DP camps with the total of 102 elementary schools, 35 Gymnasia (high schools), 43 trade schools, 1 university, 1 college (See *Ukrainian Internet Encyclopedia*).If a camp did not have a high school, then the students attended schools in camps that had them, and lived in dormitories there. Historian Orest Subtelny provides the following data for the 80 Ukrainian camps in the American zone for 1946-47: 1820 theatrical performances, 1315 concerts, and 2044 lectures. (During 1945-1948, Ukrainian refugees published over 230 periodicals and 820 books. Easy access to cultural programs, cultural personages, and publications, even in the humble camp circumstances, often proved to be a strong factor influencing students in the graduating class to continue their education at a university.
http://www.ukrainianmuseum.org/news_030311subtelnyDPcamps.html)

Who managed best later in the New World? Students who did not miss more than a year since the lower grades of high school, and especially if they had parents with them who provided support for their children. Also, college students who either completed their degrees or were close to completion and needed only a year or two of studies in North America managed well. It was hardest for those who were 17 to 22 years old; most likely, during the war they were brought to Germany for hard labor, thus they were missing at least three years of normal schooling. By 1948, some of these students married just before they went overseas; then, in the New World, not many of them could afford to go to night school while supporting a family. Thus, many talented young people simply did not develop to their full potential.

This was especially true for many extremely talented girls who were 15-17 years old at the time, and did not continue their education in college in North America. However, this was also partly due to the trend of the times: in the early 1950s, fewer than half of American and Canadian girls obtained a university education. Several of the girls from our Gymnasium, who were A+ students, did not go to college in the US. In fact, one of them committed suicide in the US, and I often wondered whether her deep depression wasn't so much due to her war experiences, as well as the fact that her life in the U.S. was limited to working in a shop in order to help her family.

Photo 57-19. The 1947 graduating class and their teachers in Neu-Ulm; every year the graduating students took their Gymnasium finals and received a traditional certificate of "maturity" ("matura"), a graduation diploma

Extracurricular Activities
There was one piano in the camp and two of us managed to practice on it, one hour a day and have our piano lessons, as well. The piano was at a makeshift radio station, reaching

only the camp residents. Somehow, I was given an opportunity to announce some programs or recite poetry on the air. In my Diary for 25 January 1948, I noted that I recited two poems by Lesia Ukrayinka; on another day, it was a verse drama by her. This was probably my first association with dramatic text as literature in performance. Later, in my adult life, this developed into serious study of drama. I enjoyed learning to use voice and reciting literary works. I observed that using the human voice artistically, is similar to performing on the piano—one has to understand the given work first, and only then express it. From time to time, I also performed on the piano for the radio station. My friend Tania Prushynska (Tkachenko) was the other student practicing the piano there. She later became a pianist and a leading piano teacher at Toronto's Royal Conservatory of Music. There was also a chess club in the camp, and Tania was one of the two girls in it. The club participated in tournaments outside the camp, and often brought trophies home.

Youngsters also had an opportunity to study art. In 1946, or so, a man called Mykola Zhyvaho arrived with his beautiful daughter Lesia/Larissa. He was an artist and taught art at the Gymnasium, as well as privately, while his daughter (who was also very talented in art) attended our high school, two grades above me. Both Zhyvahos were very strikingly attractive (both were tall, had shiny black hair, and truly dark-brown eyes), and had an aura of mystery about them. After a year or so, Mr. Zhyvaho became ill and was taken to a sanatorium, while Larissa moved to be with her mother, in another city. This happened so suddenly that our schoolmates did not miss an opportunity to discuss numerous scenarios of political intrigue and kidnapping. I did not hear about the Zhyvahos after they disappeared from our horizon. However, about 10 years later, Boris Pasternak's book *Doctor Zhivago* certainly brought to mind several similarities with "our" Zhyvahos (inc. Larissa Zhyvaho). This was especially obvious, since the surname, while written in Ukrainian, would be pronounced "Zhivago" in Russian.(See Addendum to Chapter 3 in reference to Ukrainian vs. Russian alphabets).

Our school held concerts and special programs dedicated to various writers or associated with sports activities. This provided my classmates and me an opportunity to sing in a choir, learn artistic recitation of poetry, or participate in calisthenics competitions. It was while we stayed at the DP camp, that I also attended opera for the first time, and saw *Rigoletto* at the Ulm Opera House. Although regular tickets were too expensive for refugees, my mother obtained passes from a violinist friend in the camp (Mr. Roman Sohor, who played in the Ulm Symphony Orchestra). Later, a Ukrainian Opera Ensemble from another camp visited our camp with several operas performed in Ukrainian, Italian, or French by well-known singers from pre-war Kyiv and Lviv Ukrainian opera houses.

We had an excellent theater ensemble ("Zahrava"), with first-rate actors and a great ballet troupe (after all, our camp was named in honor of the theater director Max Reinhardt!). In addition, we had the opportunity to see various productions performed by visiting Ukrainian theaters from other camps, especially two directed by outstanding artistic directors, Volodymyr Blavatsky (Ensemble of Ukrainian Actors) and Yosyp Hirniak (Theater Studio). Among more than a dozen plays that they staged in our camp, I managed to see Lesia Ukrayinka's *The Stone Host*, Mykola Khvyliovy's *Mother and I*, Kost Hupalo's *Triumph of Prosecutor Dalsky*, Yuriy Kosach's *The Enemy*, as well as Ilarion Cholhan's *A Ukrainian Night's Dream* (yes, it is "Night", not "Knight"!).

In my Diary (for 28 January 1947) I found my first written drama criticism, stating that the satire in the latter play was effective, but the scene in Paris was unconvincing. I also enjoyed the opportunity to see well-known international plays, although at the time I didn't know anything about the writers or the plays. I was able to see such classics as Goldoni's *The Servant of Two Masters*, Ibsen's *When We Dead Awaken*, Anouilh's *Antigone*, and Philip Ridley's *The Fastest Train in the Universe*. The latter play really terrified me with the speeding ghost train; this little critic could not hold back several loud expressions of fear! The foreign language plays were translated into Ukrainian and performed either by our own camp theater or other touring groups.

Photo 58-19. I, in Neu-Ulm DP camp, in 1947

It seemed that we could see any good play, and read any book that we could get hold of in that postwar situation. However, from time to time, a most unusual exclusion to that generalization would crop up, caused by none other than the Soviet representatives. Their repatriation officials in post-war Germany were trying to control not only the fate of the refugees, but also *what the refugees read.* The British author George Orwell, in his 1945 book *Animal Farm* (which was soon hailed as one of the best English language books of the twentieth century), satirically depicted Soviet leaders (Lenin, Stalin, and others), their tyranny, corruption, and their blatant falsehoods. Orwell actually feared for the Western democracies, that they were falling prey to Soviet propaganda, and that it had even influenced the British government in an effort to suppress criticism of the USSR. Orwell's book was translated into Ukrainian (by Ivan Cherniatynsky, pen name of historian Ihor Shevchenko), and had a special introduction written for that edition by the author. The book was published in 1947, in a Ukrainian DP camp.

The Soviet Repatriation Commission demanded that the American representatives confiscate and hand over to them all copies of the Ukrainian translation. Typically of the Allies, the Americans complied (I could never understand why) and the

Soviets then quickly destroyed the books that they were able to collect. The Commission feared (quite correctly!) that the book would only remind the refugees of Soviet life and horrors, and keep them from returning to a living hell in the Soviet Union. I held on to my copy of this first Ukrainian translation of *Animal Farm* (1947) and was looking forward to reading it in the original.

In 2012, Andrea Chalupa, a Washington journalist, summarized the facts about the confiscation of the translation.
http://www.theatlantic.com/entertainment/archive/2012/03/how-animal-farm-gave-hope-to-stalins-refugees/253831/
(Read on 2/28/2015, 17:55)

59-19. Cover page of the Ukrainian translation of Animal Farm by George Orwell (1947)

On the whole, my friends and I, tried to take advantage of the availability of books in any language, of seeing plays and operas that were staged in our camp, participate in sports, pursue music, dance and other activities appropriate for our age. There was something in the atmosphere inspiring us to enjoy the moment. Perhaps, this was our coping mechanism. My friends and I were happy, even though we never knew what the following week would bring in terms of the international situation that could determine our future. Our schooling system and the variety of available extracurricular activities were able to take us out of the cramped rooms with no tables to write on, nor chairs to sit on. We were exposed to numerous literary and artistic works, theories, and outstanding people. Thanks to all our activities, we were able to be aware of our short-term goals and also achieve them. This was an important psychological factor.

Yes, there was a certain type of intensity in our strong desire to enjoy the present, not knowing what was awaiting us tomorrow. And still, we were always aware of those classmates who had no parents, nor any family. In my class, there were three boys named Yuriy. The 6th of May is St. Yuriy's Day (St. George's Day).Girls from my class always went then to pick forget-me-nots (which were in full bloom then), and presented them only to the one Yuriy (Y.T.) who had no parents around; he lived with his older sister and aunt, and always appeared to be rather sad or melancholic. Somehow we felt it was our duty to make him feel appreciated (it helped, too, that he had deep blue eyes and the longest eyelashes ever!). We continued this ritual annually. Yuriy also had several family friends who cared for him; someone even managed to get him the nicest hand-embroidered Ukrainian shirt. It was an eye-catcher on the stage at any concert in which he participated.

Photo 60-19. Sailor's Dance that my group performed on Mother's Day in 1947

Both the school and Scouting-Plast often held various programs with different groups singing, dancing, reciting poetry, or participating in gymnastics meets, excursions, etc.

Scouting

Although I was not able to join Ukrainian Scouting (Plast) while still living in Ukraine (under two foreign occupations), paradoxically, I was given that opportunity only in a refugee Displaced Person's camp. Besides having regular weekly meetings, we also had excursions to important nature or cultural sites nearby, or went hiking and camping. We had Scouts of all ages; at first, I was a Brownie (my troop was called "Swans").According do my Diary, when I turned 12, I became a real Scout, joined a troop called "Kalyna" (Guelder Rose), and was elected troop leader.

Photo 61-19. Ukrainian Scouts and Cub Scouts in the Ukrainian DP camp in Reinhardt-Kaserne in Neu-Ulm, Germany (1948)

My family and I left the camp in 1948, when we had to move to Munich, to a camp for pre-departure candidates to overseas countries. Some of my friends, who stayed longer in Neu-Ulm, had more opportunities to interact with the local German population. By the end of 1948, they were all forced to leave the camp (apparently IRO completed its primary assignment) and had to move to private quarters and live among the Germans. After the camps were closed down, my younger friend Roman V. (who stayed in Germany a year longer than I) was in closer contact with local Germans. He remembers that most of them

135

Photo 62-19. At a Ukrainian Scouts camp, sponsored by IRO (1947)
I sit in the front.

treated the DPs with contempt. After all, to many of them, we were their former slaves! The Nazis considered Slavic nationalities to be *Untermenschen* vs. "Aryans"/Germans who claimed to be *Übermenschen*! This attitude must have rubbed off on many non-Nazis as well. Many Germans resented the fact that Germany's recent enemies (the Allies) were providing food to the refugees. Roman V. remembers seeing a mass meeting that the Germans held in Ulm, demanding that all refugees leave Germany.

However, despite such unpleasant events, most youngsters and many adults felt rather hopeful about an improvement in the international political situation. In our Christmas or Easter card greetings, the usual expressions of seasonal wishes always ended with "may we meet soon in an independent Ukraine," or "let's meet soon in golden-domed Kyiv, in a free Ukraine" (referring to the many Ukrainian golden-domed churches in Kyiv). No wonder that many Easter cards had printed texts like "Christ Has Risen" (Ukrainian Easter greeting) with the response "Ukraine Shall Rise, Too!"

After all, the Nazis were defeated and the war ended, so wouldn't the Russian occupation of Ukraine end one day, too? For the third time in the twentieth century, Russia (first czarist, then communist, twice) used some type of pretense or cover-up in order to occupy Ukraine: in 1914, 1939, and 1945. No one would have believed that the same political and military tactics against Ukraine would be repeated in the year 2014! We all hoped that WWII would end the Russian desire for their neighbor's land, home, and people!

No matter how painful it was to move further and further away from Ukraine, we all knew that we had to keep on going further WEST, even if we had to leave Europe altogether. Since we survived the war, and survived both the Russian and the Nazi occupations and atrocities, we felt that we had a duty to *remember* what happened during WWII, to remember the facts. We were painfully aware that youngsters in Ukraine under the Soviets did not have access to historical data about foreign occupations, so we felt duty-bound to remember and protect all such information. Only in the West would we be able to do this. This argument made our parting with Europe a little easier.

Although I missed my brother, I was hoping that we would meet soon. I felt that I was fortunate to have what I had, and especially that I had my parents around. After all, many of my classmates did not! Mother said that my attitude stemmed from the two *right shoes* that I was left with during the war, and that is why I was always ready to start off on the right foot.

Chapter 20

UNEXPECTED ENCOUNTERS
AND KIND DEEDS

Wars do not destroy people's humanity, which can bloom even in the most harrowing and atrocious circumstances.

During our chaotic refugee wanderings to and fro, there were many fortunate encounters with complete strangers. For example, I experienced three such moments with people who saved me from being shot (as described previously). There were also the kind strangers who returned our lost belongings, representing a great proportion of what we possessed while leading the life of nomads. There were also many unusual situations due to chance encounters with friends or family.

   * During our post-Strasshof period, in our continued relocations by freight trains to one city or another, my family was fortunate to be released unexpectedly from the rigors of Nazi camp life. This happened only because, by chance, we had learned the whereabouts of our friends, the Duwalo family, and they, in turn, were able to get a German Bauer/farmer to send us the much-needed affidavit to come to work for him. We were able to leave the camps, thanks to the Duwalos, who were our family's friends from our hometown. There was another tie between us: Mrs. Irena Duwalo was my father's former student at the Stryi Teachers College.

* It was by a strange coincidence that someone gave us the address of our former dentist, Dr. Halyna Skoretska, who at the time was sent to work in Vienna. She, in turn, knew where my mother's sister and brother were staying in Semmering (Austria), whom we were soon able to join.

* Our paths crossed with the Boyanivsky/Bojaniwsky family several times in Slovakia and in Germany. Mrs. Boyanivska was also my father's former student at the Zolochiv Teachers College. When Father could not get a job in Austria, her husband found jobs for my father and my two uncles in Pössneck, Thuringia.

* When we left Semmering to go to Father's new job in Thuringia, we were forced to stop in Würzburg. Father went to the mayor's office to inquire where we could spend a day or two. We were directed to a certain house that had been bombed, and the owners were absent; we were told that another refugee family was permitted to stay in the house itself, but we could make use of the garage. We went there, and to our surprise, we met the Mudry family. Mrs. Mudra also happened to have been my father's former student at the Women's Teacher's College in Zolochiv. Not only that, Mrs. Mudra was now on the way to join her sister, Mrs. Boyanivska. The Mudry family had a very small truck and insisted that we join them. Our new saviors refused to leave without helping my father and our extended family. They offered to share the limited space on the small truck with all eight of us (which included my Uncle Lonhyn, my Aunt Sofia's family and her dental assistant Rozalia). We loaded our belongings onto the small "Praha" truck. It couldn't manage going up even a hint of a hill; it huffed and puffed so much that we all needed to get off and push the truck. In this manner, we passed through several cities and towns, making short stops for the night. We also halted whenever some poor soul along the way had a terrible toothache and begged dentist Aunt Sofia to fix a dental problem. I can still visualize the simple wooden folding chair that she had with her. It had detachable armrests and a head support. Aunt Sofia had a drill with a dental wheel, which she worked mechanically with her foot. It was amazing how quickly she could set up her "dental office," whether in the middle of a city square or a field.

* In that very same city of Würzburg (Germany), Father was walking down a city street one day when he passed a lady with a teenage daughter. Seconds later, stunned, he turned around, and so did they: there was my father's sister-in-law and her daughter – Aunt Edi and Lida (I am grateful to Lida for reminding me of that event!). What were the odds for such a meeting in a strange city, as well as a strange country? And what joy it brought all of us! We were able to be with them for two whole days, and then they had to continue on their journey, since they were travelling with Aunt Edi's side of the family. Somehow, I was hoping that we would continue our wanderings together. Since my brother was not with us, I missed him terribly and always craved time with other family members closer to my own age. But at the time, the communists were apparently only a day's distance from Würzburg, so all refugees were eager to get away as quickly as possible.

* After the war, most of the refugees (as well as our family) from Eastern Europe stayed in Displaced Persons camps (or "DP" camps). We were provided with some food and clothing there, through the kindness of American aid organizations and American programs administered by UNRRA and IRO. But the meals were very limited in scope and calories. Then one day, two of my father's former students (the composer Mykhailo Haivoronsky, living in New York, Mr. Fodchuk, a teacher in Edmonton, Canada), and my grandparent' young theologian friend from the 1920s (Rev. John Bala) sent us a taste of unexpected luxury: CARE packages. These kind souls had somehow learned of our family's fate and paid for packages containing such post-war precious delicacies as two chocolate bars, two cans of SPAM, powdered milk, cocoa, and a roll of "Life Savers" candy. When the meaning of the brand name "Life Savers" was translated, the candies soon attracted much public attention in the camp: some people at first treated it literally as a medication able to save a life! Even if most refugees there did not take the name of the candies seriously, it certainly did bring a ray of joy, if not hope and laughter.

Dear Reader: If you ever have a chance to send a CARE package to a refugee, do it! It provides not just nutrition for the body, but also hope for the soul, showing that somewhere, there are people who actually care!

* In the first half of 1948, my family received a letter from two people whom Mother knew 30 years earlier: Anna and

Antin Oleksiuk from Winnipeg, Canada. Anna Oleksiuk was one of the poor orphans whom my grandmother had taken in and later gave her blessing to marry Antin, a rich sweetheart, before they left for Canada in the early 1920s. Now the Oleksiuks wanted to help the daughter and granddaughter of their benefactor. But Mr. Oleksiuk had lost his job in the early months of 1948, and kept asking around among his friends where to find work, since otherwise he would not be able to help us and be our sponsor. Hearing that, his friends (many of whom still remembered my grandparents) set up a whole network in Winnipeg to help him get a job. He was soon working again and was able to send us the necessary sponsorship papers.

The circle of good deeds was completed.

No good deed is really forgotten! It keeps going around and around, in a circle, until it finds a spot where it is recreated.

Chapter 21

WHERE TO NOW?

While younger children viewed camp life as our new "virtual world," most of my friends and classmates actually *enjoyed* our daily life as it was: we worked hard in school, we participated in all types of extracurricular activities, we played, appreciated and breathed the air that life offered us. And – we always had many friends around us! It not only was better than the life *during the war* (and in a strange land, too!), it had a substance and order, and prepared us for a future, for which we now had more realistic hopes. After all, we were *survivors*.

For adults, it was a different story. Although they were hoping to see Russia pushed back to its own territory, and the other Soviet republics freed, the adults never knew what the following week would bring in terms of the international situation. The refugees were especially distressed whether the Allies would give in to the Russian pressure demanding the "return" of all who had lived in the territories that the Soviets occupied in 1945. And what would happen to us if the Russians would soon occupy Western Europe too?

When Europe in general, and Germany in particular, was partitioned in 1945, the Russians had a free hand to do whatever they wanted on the eastern side of the Berlin Wall, and also to make demands in reference to the parts of the western side under American, British, and French administrations. The Allies always seemed to give in to the Russians.

Most refugees were quite pessimistic about the length of time Moscow would be allowed to dominate and dictate in the countries of Eastern Europe. Can't the western countries see what was happening? Russia's hand was seen in the sudden disappearances of leading personalities; while some of them were never heard of again, others suddenly appeared in the USSR. Such disappearances lead to horror stories of kidnappings by the Soviets, or stories of spies sent by the Soviets to live among us in the camps.

But how long could refugees stay in DP camps in these three zones, on the ruins of Germany and Austria? There was always the threat that the communists in general, and Russians in particular, would reach across the divide and grab more land, or at least more people. Information about the terrible fates of those who were repatriated was like a sword hanging over the heads of refugees, and so was the knowledge of the suffering of those sent to GULAGs on fabricated charges. Some of the forcefully repatriated would, at best, be able to stay in their country, if not in their home city. However, they would not have the same rights to speak and study in their own language and practice their own religion, while the Russians did. And how many would be arrested and sent to Siberia? While considering such possibilities, some refugees chose suicide. Nevertheless, out of the roughly 2 million Ukrainian refugees, most were actually repatriated and by force; only about 200,000 remained in the western zones of Germany under the Allies.

People in the camps were usually pessimistic about the Soviets staying only on the eastern side of the Berlin Wall. Refugees did not feel safe in West Germany (as it was called then), even though the Nazis were defeated. Where else could we go? Perhaps, even all the way across the ocean? Most people were willing to cross the ocean, to any country that would take them, and to work in any job that they could get — as long as it was far, far away from communism and from Moscow's constant grabbing of new territories. Pity the relatives who were locked behind the Iron Curtain for decades and decades, with no chance to leave the "prison of nations" even for a short visit to the West. Not only that, they were often punished in some way for having relatives in the "outside world."

In order to be ready to emigrate, many adults also seriously studied foreign languages (French, English, or Spanish). Younger people, studying at The Ukrainian Free University in Munich, or at German universities, acquired various professions, hoping that they would be able to work in those fields in the countries willing to take them. At that time, about two thousand young Ukrainians attended universities. A large percentage of the 18-25-years-olds, who had been brought to Germany as forced slave-laborers before they could complete their schooling, tried to learn a trade. Many countries in the New World wanted skilled and unskilled workers (rather than professionals), and they eagerly accepted these young people. The primary focus for most adults was to find some overseas country willing to take them *as soon as possible*. For this to happen, adults had to be prepared to work in any type of job. Such countries as Brazil, Argentina, and Canada wanted *only manual/blue collar* laborers. Therefore, in our camp, countless training courses were organized for people to acquire some manual know-how in photography, beekeeping, farming, tanning, or sewing.

Both my parents accepted the need to train in new occupations. Father tried to learn beekeeping and tanning. He was 64, and was not used to working with his hands (except to hold a pen). Thus it was quite brave of him to try something completely unrelated to his profession. But it had to be done. Mother (at 52), on the other hand, being a teacher and a trained artist, took courses in retouching photographs, sewing, and drawing dress patterns. She mastered both these tasks very quickly and was able to teach others how to draw and use patterns. Such courses were organized by the Ukrainian Women's Organization (under I.R.O.'s auspices). Mother taught these skills in DP camps in several cities. It was especially important to teach something practical to the very young women who had never managed to acquire any skills or higher education before they were forcibly brought to work in Germany.

Father was close to the age of retirement, and thus he had little hope for opportunities to teach Latin in some new country. Although he knew five languages, unfortunately English was not one of them.

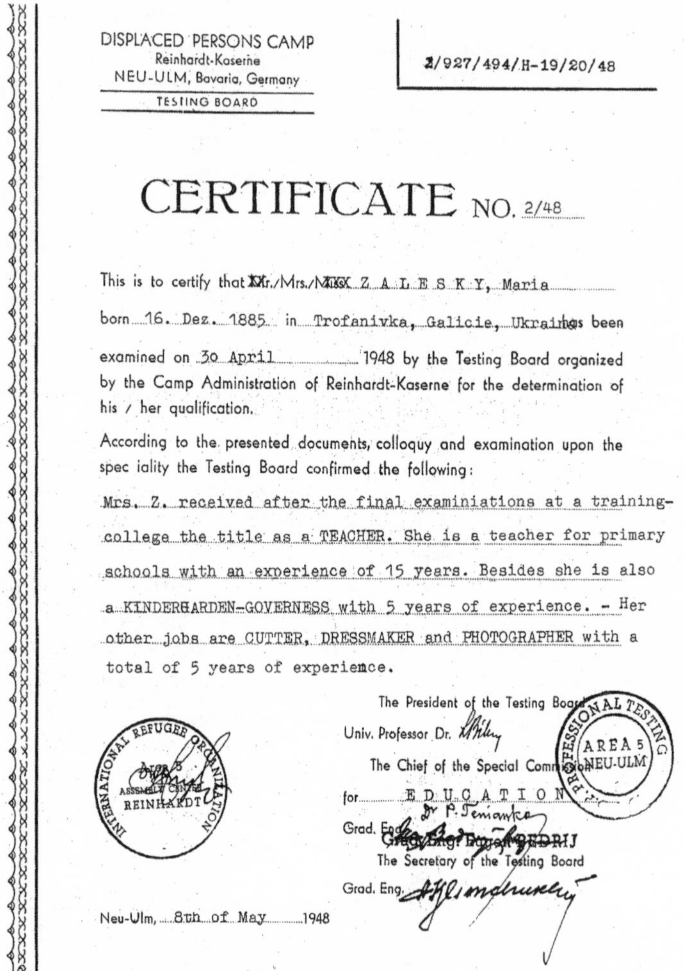

DISPLACED PERSONS CAMP
Reinhardt-Kaserne
NEU-ULM, Bavaria, Germany
TESTING BOARD

2/927/494/H-19/20/48

CERTIFICATE NO. 2/48

This is to certify that Mr./Mrs./Miss Z A L E S K Y, Maria

born 16. Dez. 1885 in Trofanivka, Galicie, Ukraine has been

examined on 30 April 1948 by the Testing Board organized by the Camp Administration of Reinhardt-Kaserne for the determination of his / her qualification.

According to the presented documents, colloquy and examination upon the spec iality the Testing Board confirmed the following:

Mrs. Z. received after the final examiniations at a training-college the title as a TEACHER. She is a teacher for primary schools with an experience of 15 years. Besides she is also a KINDERGARDEN-GOVERNESS with 5 years of experience. - Her other jobs are CUTTER, DRESSMAKER and PHOTOGRAPHER with a total of 5 years of experience.

The President of the Testing Board
Univ. Professor Dr.

The Chief of the Special Commission
for E D U C A T I O N
Dr P. Teniamko
Grad. Eng. Bedrij

The Secretary of the Testing Board
Grad. Eng.

Neu-Ulm, 8th of May 1948

INTERNATIONAL REFUGEE ORGANIZATION — AREA 5 ASSEMBLY CENTER REINHARDT

PROFESSIONAL TESTING — AREA 5 NEU-ULM

Photo 63-21. My mother's certificate attesting to her training in teaching, dressmaking, and photography

Later, I realized that it was my parents' concern for *my future* that pushed them to make the hard choices and learn new trades at their ages. They did not know where their son was, they lost close members of our family, lost their own country, their home, their professions, and now they had only me. Although they never even hinted at it, I realized later that actually all their sacrifices were for me.

Chapter 22

TAKING THE BIG STEP: ACROSS THE OCEAN

My family had only one invitation: to Canada. However, to emigrate from Europe all the way to North America was a hard step for us to take. First, there was the realization that we would be putting an ocean between my brother and us. Secondly, Aunt Sofia and her family, and Uncle Lonhyn were promised affidavits to the United States, while Uncle Osyp and cousins Chrystia and Lida Zalesky were already awaiting an affidavit to the U.S. We would be separating again from our extended family members on the western side of the Iron Curtain.

When we received our affidavit from the Oleksiuk family in Winnipeg, we had to leave Neu-Ulm and wait for further processing in Munich. On 14 April 1948, my classmates and scouting friends held a farewell party for me. Each one of them either sang a song for me or recited a poem (in my Diary, I wrote down the titles of the songs and poems). The poetry recitation was in tone with my own anthologies of poetry that I collected. It was a very emotional parting for me. I kept wondering whether I would ever see them again, or if I would ever see some of our family members.

But it took another four or five months before we held the Canadian visa in our hands. For some reason, this procedure was not only lengthy, but also required that we stay at the Funk-Kaserne camp in Munich; it was a transit camp for all nationalities awaiting departure to other foreign countries. This time, we resided in one large room with several other families, and we had two bunk beds. Our neighbor on the next bed was Miss Teklia (or Paniela Teklia), a Lithuanian high-school teacher. She had the best location since her bed was in the corner, providing her at least some semblance of privacy. Both she and I had the top bunk beds, so we could hold conversations while in in our respective beds. Not only did we have many pleasant discussions, but she also taught me some rudimentary Lithuanian. I enjoyed fooling her friends when they came asking for her, and I'd calmly reply in Lithuanian "Panelēs Teklēs nēra namuose" [Miss Teklia is not at home] or similar statements.

The waiting from one appointment to another made me restless. I heard that in our new camp there was a job offering for a student, so I applied. The administration needed a messenger to carry letters and orders to camp offices housed in several large buildings. Faxes had not been invented yet, and numerous offices serving several thousand refugees had to be kept informed somehow, so 4-6 times a day I ran my errands across the campus to different buildings. While I awaited new messages, I sat at a desk reading books. There was no real library in this camp, except for a makeshift one that consisted of incidental books that people donated before leaving the country. I discovered an unusual selection of literature; thus, I read an American classic in the German language; a Russian classic in Ukrainian, a Ukrainian translation of Dostoyevsky's *Crime and Punishment* (however, the translation had a title meaning 'Guilt and Punishment'). When I got hold of a German translation of J.F. Cooper's *The Last of the Mohicans*, I was happy that at least one book was about North America. According to my Diary, I also read several Ukrainian writers: verse dramas by Lesia Ukrayinka, and Stefan Liubomyrsky's heroic suspense stories (popular among teenagers then) about the Ukrainian underground fighting the Nazis and the communists, a reality that was still so painfully near for all of us.

Until our visa arrived, I worked at that office four hours a day, for two months. I was paid some pocket money, and also received a working person's meals, which was a great help to my family. Most importantly, I had an opportunity to read quite a few books. All in all, my first employment certainly proved to be worthwhile in all respects.

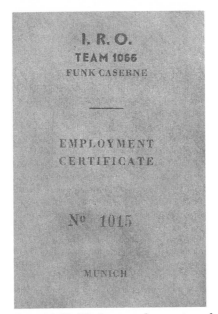

Photo 64-22. My first employment card

Just prior to our departure, we took the train to Neu-Ulm to visit Aunt Sofia and her family, to say farewell, before the ocean was to separate us.

The camp administration tried to alleviate the obvious fear of the unknown that the future emigrants to North America (as well as to other continents) had. There was a Ukrainian Youth Committee that organized a dance for young people who were leaving on 9 September 1948. I went with some friends (accompanied by our parents) and stayed there for about an hour – after all, I was 13 years old already! The dance was also an opportunity to meet some of the young people who would be on the boat with us.

On the 9 September, we left by train for the port of Bremen, and stayed there for eight more days, filling out dozens of documents and reporting to several Canadian representatives. On 17 September 1948, we said farewell to Europe, and hopefully to all the darkness that WWII had brought my family and my country. We were facing a new continent, with our three suitcases representing all our worldly belongings.

Photo 65-22. My family's Canadian immigration visa

We sailed on the SS *Samaria* of the Cunard White Star Line. The ship used to be a passenger ship, later converted to transporting soldiers, and after the war, it served tourists as well as refugees. *Samaria* was a gigantic and pleasant ship, with the top painted white, and the bottom black. In my Diary, I described the ship's six levels -- the Promenade (P), and levels A, B, C, D, and E – and wrote a comment that "it feels like a labyrinth." There were numerous large and small halls designed for different purposes, from concert halls to nooks and crannies for writing letters. I was overjoyed to see two pianos and a large library.

*Photo 66-22. The promises a train makes! My parents and I,
leaving Munich for the port of Bremen.*

On each level there was a post office, pharmacy, and a clinic.
Levels P, A, B, and C had cabins for 6-10 people, while those on
level E had large halls sleeping 150-300 people. My family was
assigned to level E. It definitely was the worst level for passengers
experiencing seasickness, especially with the storms and high waves
that we encountered. Since we were housed in this huge hall with
beds that were nailed to the floor, we had little chance for personal
discussions or family time. There were always crowds and crowds
around us.

During the day, we were able to go to the upper levels to see
the sky and the sea, and escape the worst effects of the up-and-

down movements of the ship, caused by the stormy waves. Still, even on the upper levels of the ship, many passengers did not feel that they were functioning normally. However, since there were so many people my age, whom I knew, we were constantly on the go.

Among the passengers, we had a very large Ukrainian group, and since Ukrainians love to sing, we immediately formed a choir. It was the only choir on the ship. We were happy to be singing, since then we did not feel the rocking effects of the ship so much. I sang as an alto. We gave two or three concerts during our 11-day trip. There was a well-known tenor soloist on board (whose name now escapes me), who sang with the choir and performed individual solos. There was also a large group of Ukrainian Scouts, as well as Scouts of other nationalities, with whom we planned to hold joint programs.

As a child of 6 or 7, I often tried to imagine what it might look and feel like to pass from one hemisphere to another. I felt that there must be a dividing line, something like an invisible meridian. Going from the hemisphere that had daytime, one would pass an invisible line straight into the darkness of the night in the other hemisphere. I felt that this dividing line should be somewhere in the middle of the ocean. At the age of 13, of course, I knew a little better, but when our ship, the SS *Samaria*, was crossing the ocean, I longingly remembered my theory and unsuccessfully looked for that dividing meridian.

Just before we reached the North American continent, I went to wash my hands in a large "Ladies Room." When I opened the door, a few girls (aged 10 or so) ran out giggling. For a few seconds, I didn't understand why. Then, when I tried opening the doors of half a dozen stalls, I understood: the girls had locked them all from the inside and then crawled out. Since we were facing a rather stressful moment of setting foot on a new continent, that action by the girls must have been an attempt to fight the fear of the unknown. I had to crawl inside a stall in order to use the facility. Afterwards, I unlocked the door and left it ajar.

We arrived in Quebec City, Canada, on 28 September 1948. It must have been at sunset, since everything seemed to glow in gold. On the embankment we were facing, there was a multitude of trees with colorful leaves of gold and orange hues. In that part of Canada, autumn was already in its full glory, creating a most welcoming feeling! This was Canadian Indian summer at its peak.

It took us three days by train to reach Winnipeg, Manitoba. However we were still under the spell of our first look at North America. No other city could have looked as enchanting as Quebec City did, in the embrace of the setting sun's rays.

While on the train, I felt a repeat of the same hopeful trepidation as on my train trip in 1941. There was so much of the unexpected to expect.

Now, I had to be ready for a new continent and a new country – one where the borders were not shifting, and bombs were not about to fall.

If only countries would stay within their own borders and stop invading their neighbors!

I had survived WWII, so I remained hopeful and cheerful.
I was ready for my future.
And, I made certain to guard both my shoes this time.

The rhythm of the wheels, with its constant "na-pev-no, na-pev-no, na-pev-no!" felt as if it were pointing to the future on this side of the ocean. This time, there was no hesitation in the first syllable. It was for certain.
And what exactly was it predicting for me this time?

BORDERS, BOMBS, AND... TWO RIGHT SHOES

World War II brought many European countries tremendous suffering, as well as enormous losses of life and territory. But the end of the war did not stop this loss. From the end of WWII through 1991, the number of victims of the Soviet regime decreased, but did not end. Imprisonment, executions, GULAGs, and exile to Siberia continued.

In 2009, the European Parliament passed a resolution to hold a
European Day of Remembrance for the Victims
of Stalinism and Nazism.
The commemoration was to be repeated each year
on 23 August
(commemorating the day the Stalin-Hitler Pact of 1939
was signed).

*Considering the future rather than the painful events of the past,
the Ukrainian "The First of December Group,"
consisting of statesmen and intellectuals, called upon Ukrainians:*

LET US NOT FORGET, BUT REMEMBER TO FORGIVE.

"LET US NOT CULTIVATE INIQUITY AND HATRED
AGAINST
CONSCIOUS OR UNCONSCIOUS INJUSTICES AGAINST US."
"НЕ ПЛЕКАЙМО ЗЛА І НЕНАВИСТІ
ЗА СВІДОМІ ТА НЕСВІДОМІ КРИВДИ ПРОТИ НАС."

From The "Ukrainian Charter of a Free Person"
"The First of December Group" in Ukraine, in 2012.
www.day.kiev.ua/uk/video/ukrayinska-hartiya-vilnoyi-lyudini
(Den', Dec. 8, 2012)
(Read on 12/15/2012 11:16.)

PART TWO

FACTS BEHIND AND BEYOND
MY JOURNEY

*Supplemental historical data and background information
on events and my family's war experiences described in Part I*

Chapter 23

NOTES

THE SVITOVYD STORY

Photo 67-23. The Svitovyd stone statue, c. ninth century, found in Ukraine in 1848 near the Zbruch River; in 1851, taken to a museum in Krakow, Poland (Photo: courtesy of Vsevolod Onyshkevych)

In Part I, I describe some of my family's experiences, which ensued from historical situations and wars that occurred a century or two earlier. Several events caused many Ukrainians, from the regions taken by the Russian Empire, to cross the Zbruch River (a tributary of the Dnister River), in order to flee a repressive regime and find haven in the west. They undertook their escape journey in order to protect their freedoms, particularly when foreign military forces were trying to take away these freedoms.

Centuries passed, political forces and empires coming from the west alternated several times with those from the eastern neighbor, who reappeared on Ukraine's doorstep with frequent regularity. The Zbruch River served as part of a political border between the Russian and Austrian, or Russian and Polish regimes ruling over Ukrainian territories from 1793 to 1939.

The Story of the Svitovyd Statue (or the Zbruch Idol)

In 1848, an 8-and-a-half-foot limestone statue of Svitovyd was found in the Zbruch River area, near the village of Lychkivtsi, close to the town of Husiatyn (in the Podillia region of Ukraine). This stone sculpture, from the ninth century (originating during the Kyivan Rus period), has four front-sides, with a depiction of a human face on each one. While each side faces a different part of the world, all four figures have their backs towards each other, guarding and protecting each other, while jointly sharing and standing under one hat, i.e. one ruler.

There are various interpretations of the symbolism of the four figures, as well the various tiers. One theory claims the figures were early Slavic deities. Another theory considers that each tier represents different realities: the top tier is that of pagan gods (with a bugle, a sabre, and a steed) and the lowest – the underworld, while the middle one stands for the human world (represented by two women and two men).

When the early Ukrainian state in Kyiv officially accepted Christianity in the tenth century, most of the statues from the pagan period were destroyed, usually being thrown into rivers. One theory holds that this must have been also the fate of the Svitovyd. An alternative theory suggests that the statue stood near the Zbruch River, and was later covered by the waters of this meandering river.

The statue seems to stand almost as a historical record of the life and values of the people living in the Zbruch valley at the time. Still, with all the eyes of its four upper figures (had they been alive), the statue would have "registered" the many invaders who crossed this river to claim the rich lands of ancient Ukraine: a Slavic tribe coming from the west, Tatars from the south, and a neighboring clan from the north-east. All of them sought to conquer the lands on both sides of the Zbruch. The invaders would come, temporarily occupy the land and attempt to rule over the local residents, intending not only to eradicate their freedoms but their identity as well.

After the statue was found on the banks of the Zbruch in the nineteenth century, it was taken to a museum in Krakow, where it continues to stand, isolated from all the historical events and concerns of the last 150 years.

Perhaps it is easier on Svitovyd's all-seeing eyes that it was not forced to witness all the gruesome events that Ukraine had to face in the twentieth century and beyond.

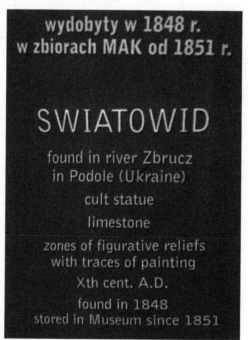

Photo 68-23. A plaque in the Krakow Museum of Art
(Photo: Courtesy of Vsevolod Onyshkevych)

Even in the twentieth century, Svitovyd remained a presence in the subconscious of the people near the Zbruch River. My mother described how, in her younger years, together with her siblings and friends, she would go on excursions to the place where the Svitovyd statue was found. She referred to the statue as if it still stood on the banks of the Zbruch during her lifetime, although it was taken to Poland 44 years before she was born. The statue has become identified with the Zbruch River and all that it signifies in the historical and political events of Ukraine, the local people's individual lives, and particularly, as an important border between the West and the East.

To the Ukrainian residents living in the area of the Zbruch and even beyond it, the two sides of the river represented freedom and individual choice (the western sides) versus totalitarianism (the eastern side). This river was most firmly associated with the fate of my maternal ancestors. The story is particularly closely entwined with the recurring Russian pursuit of western Ukrainian lands (in 1914, 1939, and 1945), as well as the Russian desire to enforce their own religion, language, and identity on Ukrainians throughout the last four centuries. Just how strong were some of the local ties to the Svitovyd may be well seen in the fact that my mother chose for her gravestone a stone cross with four facial sides, reminiscent of the Svitovyd statue.

Notes to Chapter 1

A TRAIN RIDE, WOLVES, AND A FUNERAL

• *At the end of the eighteenth century, the territory where Ukrainians and their ancestors lived for over a millennium, and where they also constituted a majority of the population, was divided between the Austrian and the Russian empires. In 1773, in the Austrian part (administered by Poland), the Ukrainian Greco-Catholic Church had equal rights with the Polish Roman Catholic Church. In 1781, the Austrian Empire extended similar rights to all religions. The Zbruch River served as part of the borderline between the Austrian and the Russian Empires in 1773-1918, and then between Poland and the USSR in 1921-1939.*

• *Our family genealogical documents show that my maternal ancestor, Rev. Platon Shankovsky served as a Greco-Catholic priest in Cherniakhiv, in the Zhytomyr area (North East of the Zbruch River, in the Volyn region). In 1793, the Russian Empire annexed the area. Rev. Platon represented the 11th generation of Greco-Catholic priests in his family, which was granted nobility status in 1410 (as the House of Liubych, and, later, Kryvda). However, on 8 April 1793, for Ukrainians to be Greco-Catholic priests by profession, and/or hold the title of nobility, was a thorn in the eye of Russian Empress Catherine II, since both of these distinctions clearly exposed at least two differences between some Ukrainians and Russians. Catherine II demanded that all Ukrainian Greco-Catholic priests and Ukrainian nobility swear allegiance to her, and convert to the Russian Orthodox faith by the following day. Many Jews in the Russian Empire also were ordered to convert to Russian Orthodoxy, or live in the Pale of Settlement in the western parts of the Empire, beyond Russia proper. The Pale for the Volyn region was also announced in 1793. For Ukrainian Greco-Catholics living to the east of the Zbruch (then held by the Russian Empire) the choice to join the Ukrainian Orthodox Church was not a viable alternative. After all, since 1686, the Russian Orthodox Church had already forcefully absorbed the Ukrainian Orthodox faithful and claimed to represent them. It is no wonder that my ancestors and countless other Ukrainians chose so hurriedly to flee to the western parts of Ukraine. To do this they had to cross the Zbruch River.*

Rev. Platon Shankovsky, had twelve sons and four daughters. In 1793, many of the children were still very young, so, he could not consider fleeing with his family within the allotted 24-hours. Only the eldest three sons decided to risk it and cover about 185 miles to the Zbruch, in order to cross the river and reach western Ukrainian lands that were then part of the Austrian Empire. Two of the brothers, Yakiv, and Matvii, were already priests of the Ukrainian Greco-Catholic Church, and the latter was also a professor at the Lutsk Theological Seminary. The youngest of the three brothers, Toma (1769-1836), had completed his theology studies but was not ordained yet.

The three men wished to practice their own religion and serve as Greco-Catholic priests. In 1793, in the area controlled by Austria, all religions were treated equally. The Shankovsky brothers settled just west of the Zbruch River, where they, and later their male descendants, served their flock for four more generations. Our genealogical tree shows that after Rev. Platon, there were 25 more priests in the next generations of his family. When the communists came in 1939, this family tradition was interrupted, as was the opportunity for many Ukrainians to practice their Greco-Catholic faith.

The fate of Rev. Platon's other children, who were too young to cross the river by night, in order to escape from the Russian Empire, remains mostly unknown. From chance meetings between descendants of both branches, my family learned that those relatives, who remained in the Russian Empire either had to accept Russian Orthodoxy, or become Roman Catholics and claim to be Poles. Both the Russian tsars as well as the communists applied the same rule: Poles were allowed to remain Catholics, but Ukrainians were not.

Photo 69-23. My great-grandfather, Very Rev.Yakiv Shankovsky (1805-1890), was the son of Rev. Toma (the youngest of the three brothers, who managed to escape from the edicts of Catherine II against the Ukrainian Greco-Catholic Church). He served as priest, and later dean, for over 60 years in the Kopychyntsi area, near the Zbruch River.

• *This data is based primarily on genealogical information collected by my mother, Maria Shankovska Zaleska, and her cousin, Dr. Lev Shankovsky, who was a historian. In the 1920-30s, he and his father had compiled a detailed list of the preceding 10 generations of Greco-Catholic priests in the family, prior to Rev. Platon. Most of the documents with this information were lost during WWII. From all the data that I have from my family, my cousin Martha Shankovsky Shmorhun assembled a detailed genealogical tree.*

87.

Xtus positionis	Dies mortis 1915 Mensis mortuus sepultus	Numerus domus	NOMEN, COGNOMEN et Conditio Mortui	Religio Catholica	Aut alia	Sexus Masculina	Feminina	Dies Vitae	Morbus et Qualitas Morts	Adnotatio
28.	1915. 6. Novembris Sepelivit in...	67 78	Rever. Dominus Antonius Szankowski, Consiliarius Cons. Episcop., decoratus aurea cruce cum corona...			mas. cult.		81.1/2 annorum	Pneumonia	Elias Labij.

Photo 70-23. Death record of my mother's great uncle, Rev.Antonii Shankovsky (1835-1915), grandson of Rev. Toma

• *The fact that my maternal ancestors settled only a few miles from the Zbruch borderline also allowed them to personally witness not only various front-line battles taking place nearby, but also to meet several well-known Ukrainians who needed to cross the border. Perhaps the very location made the people in the Zbruch River area especially sensitive to political and historical events around them. For example, my ancestor, Rev. Toma, in his church calendar for the year 1812, noted the day when Napoleon's army marched east towards Russia. I haven't found any information about parts of Napoleon's army passing through, or close to, the Husiatyn area (situated about two hundred miles south of Napoleon's main path); still, perhaps just a group of Napoleon's scouts has been in the area and made the residents aware of the events occurring in other parts of Europe.*

• *My grandfather Shankovsky's parish and rectory were very close to the border (between the Austrian and Russian Empires), either in Chabarivka or some other village in the Husiatyn-Kopychyntsi area, where he and his brothers served. Many Ukrainian cultural leaders and personalities, who needed to cross the border illegally to visit relatives, would stop overnight at my grandfather's rectory, and then a member of the family or staff would help them to secretly cross the border. Some went east to visit their family in that part of Ukraine that was then ruled by the Russian Empire; others took the same route to go west. Among notable people going one or both ways, was the leading Ukrainian historian, Mykhailo Hrushevsky (1866-1934), who also headed the Ukrainian government, the Ukrainian Central Rada during 1917-1918. At other times, it would be his wife, who needed to cross. Stopping at my grandparents' place was also Liudmyla Shevchenko (1895-1969), grandniece of the great Ukrainian poet, Taras Shevchenko (1814-1861).*

• *Why were the Russians / Soviets in our land in the middle of the twentieth century? The historical explanation may be found in the 1939 treaty between the Soviet Union (USSR) and Nazi Germany. Based on this pact, Stalin and Hitler divided among their respective "empires" most of the eastern part of Europe. It was called the Molotov-Ribbentrop Non-Aggression Pact, or treaty of cooperation. The author of a study of the pact, Roger Moorhouse, called it "The Devils' Alliance" (2015). As a result of this treaty, most of the central and eastern Ukrainian area was to remain in the USSR, while the western-most part was to be ruled by Poland. However, within weeks Germany invaded Poland, and the Soviets took most of the western Ukrainian lands.*

Notes to Chapter 2

MY GRANDMOTHER'S CHOICE: FORGIVE THE WRONGDOER AND THEN SHELTER HIM

• *My Babunia (Grandmother) believed strongly that both sexes should have equal rights. This was in step with the then current feminist movement in Ukraine. Among the many publications with Ukrainian feminist ideas was the 1887 anthology "Pershyi Vinok" [The First Garland]. This compilation of poetry, prose, and essays by women writers, was edited by two of these writers (Natalia Kobrynska and Olena Pchilka), who also personally funded the publication of this book in Lviv. Almost a century later (in 1984), a second expanded edition was published in New York, and I had the honor to serve as its editor.*

• *Since the fifteenth century, the tumultuous history of Ukraine was characterized by many invasions and occupations by neighboring countries, particularly, Russia. In the twentieth century alone, many of my relatives (both on the paternal and maternal side) served their country in various capacities. My father was elected as representative to the Parliament of Western Ukrainian National Republic (1918-1919). It was the fate of each generation of my relatives to lose a close member of the family during various Russian invasions. In the twentieth century, the first time the Russian forces invaded western Ukrainian territory, was in 1914. Then, in 1919, my mother's brother Mykola, died while serving, as an 18-year-old volunteer in the Ukrainian Riflemen's Legion, defending independent Ukraine against Russian Bolsheviks. In 1939, the Bolshevik communists came again to western Ukrainian lands and caused my Grandfather's death. The third Russian occupation (in the guise of the Soviets) took place in 1945, after the end of WWII. It was then that my mother's brother, Uncle Yakiv Shankovsky, was arrested by the communists and sentenced to twenty years of imprisonment and hard labor in the GULAGs of Siberia; it was his punishment for providing help to Ukrainian insurgents, who were then fighting against the Nazis, as well as the Soviets. He was fortunate to spend only 10 years in Siberia, due to a partial amnesty for political prisoners after Stalin's death. In 1955, my brother Vsevolod's life was taken by the communists, in the city of Lviv.*

• *During each Russian invasion of Ukraine in the twentieth century (1914, 1939, 1945, and 2014), whether it was czarist, communist, or other form of Russian regime, they would not allow the Ukrainian Eastern Catholic, or Greco-Catholic, religion. Just as Catherine II would not permit Ukrainian Greco-Catholic religion in the lands she newly occupied in 1793, neither did later Czar Nicholas II, Stalin, nor Putin in the Crimea, in 2014. They all wanted Ukrainians to belong only to the Russian Orthodox Church, lose their own identity and language, and just become Russians.*

• *When the Soviets invaded Western Ukraine in 1939, did anyone protest? Besides thousands of Ukrainian citizens (who were then sent to Siberia for daring to protest), Andrei Sheptytsky, the Ukrainian Greco-Catholic Archbishop, wrote letters to Josef Stalin and Nikita Khrushchev strongly complaining about the mistreatment of his faithful.*

Notes to Chapter 3

WHY WERE THE COMMUNISTS RUNNING AWAY?

- *From 1920 until 1939, communists occupied central and eastern parts of Ukraine, and called it the Ukrainian Soviet Socialist Republic. Then, in 1939 they invaded the western part as well, and began ferreting out any possible previous "anti-Soviet" acts of the local Ukrainians. Although before 1939, there was a well-guarded border (Polish and Soviet) separating the two occupied parts of Ukraine from each other, bad news did manage to pass through. The worst news was about the 1932-1933 losses during the Holodomor, or Death by Starvation, organized by the Soviet government; it took the lives of 4.5 to 7 million Ukrainian peasants. Moscow refused to admit that it was confiscating grain from farmers for export, while attempting to force them to join "collective farms." In the areas of the biggest losses of life, Soviet government then brought several million Russians from Russia to settle in the eastern parts of Ukraine, many of them in the Donbas area. They were often given houses of the dead or exiled Ukrainians. While many of the Russian newcomers became industrial workers in the eastern part of Ukraine, others filled many top administrative positions in the country.*

- *Once the Soviets arrived in Western Ukraine in 1939, they immediately tried to eliminate Ukrainian activists, not just in the political sphere, but also in the cultural and administrative. The communists would arrest officials of all ranks. My cousin Christina Shypylavy's (Shepelavey's) father in-law was a community activist in a Western Ukrainian village near Buchach; he was arrested in early February 1940. Summary of his interrogation (see below) includes questions about the 1932-33 activities of the Western Ukrainian Committee to Aid Ukraine. He was asked about the following: church memorial services for the victims of the Soviet organized famine; public meetings discussing the state of affairs in the Ukrainian Soviet Socialist Republic, and searching for ways to provide food to the famine-stricken Ukrainians across the border. For heading a local committee attempting to provide aid to the victims of the famine, Mr. Shypylavy was sentenced to 20 years of hard labor. This punishment was for his activity prior to the time that the Soviets annexed the region where he lived.*

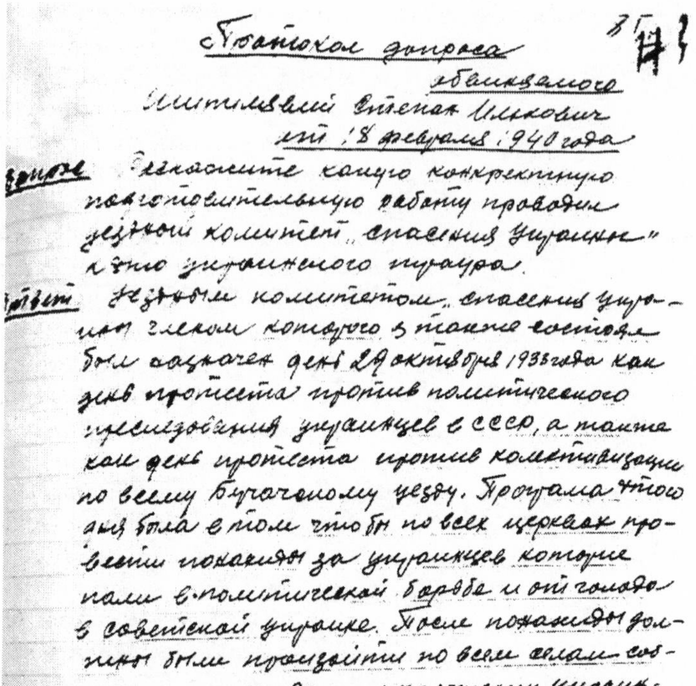
Протокол допроса
обвиняемого
Шипилявий Степан Илькович
от 18 февраля 1940 года

Вопрос: Выясните какую конкретную подготовительную работу проводил уездной комитет „спасения Украины" к дню украинского траура.

Ответ: Уездным комитетом „спасения Украины" членом которого я также состоял был назначен день 29 октября 1933 года как день протеста против политического преследования украинцев в СССР, а также как день протеста против коллективизации по всему Бучачскому уезду. Програма этого дня была в том что бы по всех церквах провести панахиды за украинцев которые пали в политической борьбе и от голода в советской Украине. После панахиды должны были произойти по всем селам собрания с докладами „о положении украинского народа на Советской Украине" как я уже говорил на предыдущем моем допросе, что в большинстве сел и в городе панахиды и собрания прошли с утверждением протеста текст которого был прислан из громадського украинского комитета „спасения украины" который существовал в г. Львове.

Вопрос: Кто руководил днем протеста на селах или на селах также были организованы местные комитеты?

Шипилявий

Photo 71-23. Document of the Interrogation of Stepan Ilkovych Shypylavy, on 18 February 1940
The original handwritten text is in the Russian language.
See website of the Holodomor of 1932-1933, the Ternopil Oblast, State Archives.
http://www.archives.gov.ua/Sections/32-33/
(Accessed on 28 February 2015, 15:45)

- *Since 2014, the above website of archival government documents of Soviet arrests, interrogations, sentences, and losses of life associated with the Holodomor-Famine in 1932-33, provides data for the whole of Ukraine, as well as individually for the 17 oblasts / regions and separately for the cities of Kyiv and Sevastopol.*

- *During the last weeks of the Soviet occupation of western Ukraine in June 1941, thousands of Ukrainians (especially those suspected of being insurgents or those helping them), were exiled to Siberia's GULAGs. Then, on the last day before the Soviets retreated (on or about 21-22 June 1941), they massacred Ukrainian political prisoners. When the Nazis arrived on 22 June 1941, they decided to exploit's the local people's emotional reaction to the carnage, by inspiring interethnic hatred. "The Germans helped to circulate rumors that 'Jewish Bolsheviks' had been involved in the murders."(See Paul Robert Magocsi, A History of Ukraine. Seattle: Univ. of Washington Press, 1996; 2nd printing, 1997, p.631.)*

- *When the Soviet Army was retreating from the Nazi front on 21 June 1941, in my home town of Stryi, communist soldiers killed and / or burned to death several hundred Ukrainian and Polish political prisoners, both male and female, who had been arrested for their suspected dislike, or just lack of support of the Soviet regime. Reports of the killings describe mutilated and dismembered bodies, ears and noses lopped off, dead and / or live people hurriedly thrown into large kettles, or burned and then stuffed in the sewer system. Most of the disfigured bodies were charred beyond recognition – which was the aim of that inhumane deed—in order to hide the identity of the victims. In Stryi, from the hundreds that were killed, only 46 individuals were identifiable when the Soviets left (as reported by an eyewitness, I. Stryis'kyi, "Stryi", in "Zlochyny Komunistychnoi Moskvy v Ukrayini vliti 1941 roku," Prolog, 1960, pp. 78-81). Since the fall of the Soviet Union, numerous documents continue to be published, describing similar occurrences in most prisons in Ukraine at that time. In the neighboring Lviv region / oblast (to which Stryi currently belongs), on 22 June 1941, there were 5,424 inmates in the oblast's prisons. That day the Soviets began executing 4,140 inmates, while 1,822 were evacuated.*

(Uk.Wikipedia.orgВинищення_львівських_в%27язнів_у_ червні_1941. Read on 25 July 2016, 14:56.)

• *The infamous Katyn Massacre of 1940 symbolizes another typical Soviet modus operandi: there were 21,867 Polish victims (including some non-Poles who were Polish citizens). Among the victims were 4 to 5 thousand military officers, a large number of Polish intellectuals and artists, executed by the communists on Stalin's directive and with the approval of the Soviet Politburo. It took several decades for these facts to become widely known. (en.wikipedia.org / wiki / Katyn-massacre. Read on 28 February 2015, 16:40.)*

• *Ukrainian freedom fighters took up arms against both the Nazis and the Soviets. Since after April 1941 alone, there were 38 anti-Soviet battles and confrontations, the Soviet secret police was ordered to liquidate western Ukrainian insurgents and activists. David E. Murphy cites that from by 23 May 1941, the Soviets had "detained and loaded on freight cars for their journey into exile 11,476 persons." ("What Stalin Knew. The Enigma of Barbarossa." Yale UP, 2005, p. 34.)*

On Genocide

• *For decades, the Soviet communist regime carried out purges against educated Ukrainians: in the 1930s, they executed over 400 members of the Ukrainian Academy of Sciences, and over 350 Ukrainian writers. In 1932-33, they starved to death millions of Ukrainian farmers in the artificial famine, or Holodomor [literally "death by starvation"]. In an extreme attempt to save the lives of their own children, thousands of starving farmers abandoned them on the streets of Kharkiv, in the hope that someone might save them.*

Records of the Holodomor period, released in 2014, showed that the farmers did not accept their fate passively; there were over 900 cases of rebellion (often by armed citizens) against the Soviet confiscation of all food supplies from the local people. At the same time, the Soviet regime would not allow outsiders (even Ukrainians from just across the western border) to send food to the starving millions. In the 1930s, millions of Ukrainians were sent to Siberia, where a large number perished. Thus, the top and the bottom of the Ukrainian social pyramid were decimated, representing about a quarter of the Ukrainian population.

• *What is the correct classification of a crime when a foreign regime starves close to 20-25% of a country's population? Today, such acts have an internationally accepted name, genocide. It was Raphael Lemkin (a Polish Jew, born in Belarus, studied law at the Lviv University in Ukraine in the 1920s), who coined the term genocide. In 1941, he came to the United States, taught at Duke University, and later at Rutgers University. He served as advisor to the US Supreme Court during the Nuremberg Trial sessions (1945-46).*

• *On December 11, 1946, the UN General Assembly officially recognized the term* genocide, as one referring to the physical, as well as to cultural and linguistic aspects of the crime.

Two years later, on 9 December 1948, the Convention on the Prevention and Punishment of the Crime of Genocide (CPPCG) was adopted by the United Nations General Assembly, as General Assembly Resolution 260.

http: / / www.un.org / en / preventgenocide / adviser / pdf / osapg_analysis_framework.pdf (Read on 30 November 2014, 4:59 pm)

Raphael Lemkin's description of genocide:

• *"Genocide is directed against the national group as an entity, and the actions involved are directed against individuals, not in their individual capacity, but as members of the national group."*

• *"Genocide has two phases: one, destruction of the national pattern of the oppressed group; the other, the imposition of the national pattern of the oppressor. This imposition, in turn, may be made upon the oppressed population which is allowed to remain or upon the territory alone, after removal of the population and the colonization by the oppressor's own nationals."*

Raphael Lemkin, "Genocide," Axis Rule in Occupied Europe, 2nd ed. Lawbook Exchange: Clark, N.J., 2008. 79.

And http://en.wikipedia.org/wiki/Raphael_Lemkin *(Read on Dec. 2, 2014, 15.22, and on April 26, 2015, 11:04).*

• *In 1953, speaking in New York City, on the 20th Commemoration of the* Ukrainian Genocidal *Famine, Raphael Lemkin, in his lecture on the Holodomor, called it a Ukrainian genocide, and illustrated all its facets (cultural, religious, ethnic, and demographic).*

(http: / / www.uccla.ca / SOVIET_GENOCIDE_IN_THE_UKRAINE. pdf) (Read on Dec. 2, 2014,16:08)

Linguistic Genocide

• *Taking into account how R. Lemkin defined the Soviet multifaceted practices of genocide, using facts, one may also demonstrate a gradually enforced* linguistic genocide *of the Ukrainian language. Just as the sign on the Stryi prison was in the Russian language, so were most official documents. Enforced Russification, in terms of language and / or religion, was not a new practice by Russians. Throughout many centuries, all the Russian regimes (both the imperial and the Soviet) that occupied Ukraine, attempted to suppress the Ukrainian language by means of various prohibitions and edicts. The tsarist Valuev Edict of 1863, even proclaimed, that "there is no Ukrainian language, never was, and never shall be." They did not see the lack of logic in the claim: if it did not exist, why bother proclaiming its non-existence?*

Since the Russian czarist policies were not successful in eradicating the Ukrainian language, the communists tried a different approach. If they could not discourage the usage of the Ukrainian language, and then bring its end, perhaps they could gradually change it to resemble the Russian language?

On August 28, 1943, when the Soviets were still in the middle of the war with the Nazis, Nikita Khrushchev (at the time, head of the Communist Party of Ukraine), called a meeting of the Ukrainian Soviet government and members of the Ukrainian Academy of Sciences, in Pomirky, a village near Kharkiv. Its purpose was to discuss hurriedly new proposals for changing the rules for the Ukrainian orthography, i.e. spelling, grammar, and vocabulary. Since 1938, Khrushchev was in charge of organizing purges in Ukraine, and now organized that meeting to purge the Ukrainian language.

The meeting was not planned to be a scholarly conference of linguistic experts. However, it turned out to be an absurdist scene: Khrushchev and his commissars, in army uniforms, dictating to leading Ukrainian academicians and writers what new rules and regulations or restrictions in the Ukrainian language were to be made mandatory. The committee of language specialists were instructed to provide a set of new rules which would "secure the unity with the orthographies of the brotherly peoples of the Soviet Union, especially that of the Russian ..."

Photo 72-23. During WWII, with battles raging quite nearby, soldiers, Party leaders (on the left), Khrushchev, with Ukrainian academics and writers (on the right) at Pomirky (near the city of Kharkiv), on 28 August 1943, discussing the Communist Party's decision to introduce new rules for the Ukrainian language

• *As a result of this meeting, new directives were issued in the form of rules to be published as the new Ukrainian Orthography of 1946. Among the changes, most notable were the rules for spelling foreign words, which were to copy the Russian transliteration. There were several sadly comical results of these enforced changes, as may be seen in the following examples.*

• *They eliminated the letter "G" from the Ukrainian alphabet, keeping the Ukrainian "H" (which looks like the Russian "G"). (Perhaps, the Soviets thought: it won't do for Ukrainians to have both a "G" and an "H", while Russians have only a "G"?) Until 1946, Ukrainians pronounced "Hegel" as in the English language, while Russians would render it as "Gegel." However, the new rules forced Ukrainians to pronounce it as "Hehel." Thus, even in the mid-1990s, when the former Vice President Gore visited Ukraine, he was introduced as "Vice President Hore," creating a most embarrassing diplomatic situation.*

• *In terms of vocabulary, common Slavic words that are also found in the Russian language were approved, while typically*

Ukrainian words were often labeled "archaic," "nationalistic," or even "fascist." Artificial restrictions and directions to copy the Russian language were just the beginning. The subsequent Orthography of 1960 introduced still bolder changes and directives to bring the Ukrainian language much closer to the Russian. Those who dared to disagree were again called "nationalists" or "fascists," and soon many of them spent their years in Siberian or other Soviet GULAGs.

• *Whether during the czarist regime, or the Soviet one, edict after edict, various linguistic restrictions and changes to the Ukrainian grammar, spelling, and vocabulary, plus actual political and legal limitations placed on the use of the language, together represent a linguicide, which the U.N. considers to be a part of genocide.*

Notes to Chapter 4

ONE TYRANT FROM THE EAST AND ONE FROM THE WEST *Or WHO WAS THE CRUELEST OF THEM ALL?*

• *During WWII, both the Russians (Soviets / communists), as well as the Germans (Nazis), were foreign aggressors. Both were eager to acquire more land and food for their own people, and both needed more fighting men and converts to their respective ideologies. Both regimes wanted Ukraine's land (the Lebensraum plan) and labor force. Both invaders brought totalitarian and dictatorial regimes to the occupied lands. Both of them were xenophobic. Stalin wanted citizens of all the 14 non-Russian republics to accept communist ideology and use the Russian language, so that eventually all the conquered nations would slowly assimilate into Russian-speaking communists. Hitler claimed superiority of the German people and their race (calling it "Aryan" or Nordic), but did not wish to assimilate the conquered Slavic people, only to limit their education and turn them into slaves / serfs, while German colonists, would rule over them.*

• *Stalin and Hitler not only acted in a similar manner, they learned from each other. They both claimed that their respective parties were those of workers: the Soviets stated that they represen-*

ted workers and the proletariat, while the Nazis actually were called the National Socialist German Workers Party (i.e. the Nazi Party). Hitler learned from Stalin how to organize concentration camps, labor camps, ethnic cleansing, and how to make the best use of the colonized. The two autocratic leaders had some common interests, and therefore signed the Molotov-Ribbentrop Pact in 1939, deciding how to divide Poland and Ukraine to serve their own interests. In the early years of WWII, when some of the left-leaning Jews were running away from Germany to the areas ruled by Stalin, he had many of them caught, put them on train cars, and sent them back to Hitler to be executed in concentration camps. Then, in 1940, after some Jews had personally experienced what the Soviet regime represented, they risked everything to escape, sometimes even to the Nazi-controlled Poland.

• *When, in the 1980s, details of the Molotov-Ribbentrop Pact of 1939 became widely known, they disclosed that Hitler was pursuing projects very much in Stalin's style: liquidating people who did not conform to what the dictator demanded. After WWII, Stalin withheld his criticism of Hitler's regime – after all, they both followed a similar path. Winston Churchill grasped this similarity quite early, and is credited to have said:* "Nazism is a form of Soviet communism."

Both the Nazis and the Soviets, while they occupied Ukraine, they targeted and liquidated the same type of individuals and groups: professional people, religious and community leaders, as well as just patriotic Ukrainians and political opponents.

• *Both dictators believed they could achieve their goals by means of wars, conquests, and genocides. Stalin created a famine-genocide of Ukrainians in 1932-33 (with 4.5 to 7 million victims), and Hitler acted similarly, creating the Jewish genocide in 1943-45 (with 6 million victims). During WWII, Ukraine lost about a quarter of its population again: 5 million ethnic Ukrainians, a million of Jewish victims in the Holocaust, and about 1 million victims from other ethnic groups. The city of Kyiv illustrates the population loss most visibly: in 1940, it had close to 900 thousand inhabitants, while in 1943, only about 180 thousand.*

• *During WWII, both Russia and Germany occupied foreign countries, ruling over them and terrorizing people. Both aggressors wanted more territory, and tried to justify their actions by blindly obeying their respective extreme ideologies. Many people, who had never had a first-hand taste of the communist rule, trusted the propaganda and slogans of this ideology, without bothering to look at the reality, not to mention the facts of the Russian and the Soviet past practices.*

Similarly, people who had never been occupied by Russia and had only during WWII experienced Nazi rule (including concentration camps and persecution), would not believe that some other country could possibly be as bad as Germany. Slovaks, who themselves had already dealt with former German occupation, but had never experienced a Russian regime, thought positively about the latter as "brother Slavs." It was typical of the tragic postwar situations and events: when trying to get away from one enemy, any new enemy is expected to be not half as bad.

• While the Soviets persecuted mostly Poles and Ukrainians, either shipping them off to Siberia or executing them, Nazis arrested Jews and Gypsies first, trying to annihilate them completely. Ukrainians and Poles were considered "Untermenschen," or "inferior people," and were sent to concentration and death camps, or, at best, shipped to Germany to serve as slave laborers. The Nazis made it their priority to arrest hundreds of Ukrainian political activists. It is estimated that about 21,000 Ukrainian political prisoners were held in various Nazi concentration camps. Among them were about 2,000 members of Ukrainian Nationalist Organizations, and a large number of political, religious, cultural leaders, as well as Ukrainians from all walks of life. (See www. memory.gov.ua*)*

Notes to Chapter 5

WAS I TO BE THE 6,000,001st VICTIM?

• During WWII, the Nazis killed approximately 6 million European Jews; many local Christians risked their own lives while trying to save the threatened neighbors. After the Armenian genocide and the Holodomor, the Holocaust represented the third genocide in Europe in the twentieth century. Europe was losing

its people again. When the communist Soviet regime starved Ukrainian farmers in the Holodomor, Moscow kept denying this horrible deed, and the huge demographic loss was not documented in state statistics, because the Soviet government suppressed its next census results, for the year 1939. After the fall of the Soviet Union, names and facts were slowly collected to reconstruct the number of Ukrainians killed in the Holodomor; the current estimate is between 4.5 to 7 million.

For a long time, the world outside the Iron Curtain ignored the genocide in Ukraine. Had the Western world reacted during the Armenian genocide in 1915, perhaps Stalin would have thought twice about planning genocide of Ukrainians in 1932-33, Hitler would not have dared to start a Jewish genocide a decade later, nor would Karadzic have tried to carry out the genocide of Bosnians in the 1990s. Perpetrators of each subsequent genocide learned from the earlier ones: Stalin learned from the Ottomans, Hitler learned from Stalin, and so on.

• During 1941-1945, thousands of Ukrainians were sent to Nazi concentration camps. However, at that time, Ukraine was not an independent country, therefore, Ukrainians were often listed as Poles or Russians (since they held either Polish or Soviet citizenship), or were simply identified as "stateless." Due to this, it is almost impossible to arrive at a more exact number of Ukrainians in the Nazi camps.

• Nazis often misidentified their victims in terms of nationality. For example, the statistics of the victims at Babyn Yar [Babi Yar, in Russian], near Kyiv, is still not definitive, with the highest estimate being as high as 200,000. Jewish victims were recorded to be 33,771, although some were very likely also listed with other groups (such as communist activists or groups of professionals), bringing the total close to 50,000. At least 40,000 victims were Ukrainian, e.g.: 621 members of the Organization of Ukrainian Nationalists; there were also professors, scholars, cultural leaders, members of the Ukrainian Plast-Scouting Organization, Ukrainian Orthodox priests, and Ukrainian writers. Among the latter group of victims was Olena Teliha (one of my favorite poets when I was a teenager). She served as President of the Ukrainian Writers Union, and was the chief editor of the literary magazine "Litavry." Together with her husband and the editorial board,

she was arrested and then executed by the Nazis, on 22 February 1942, at the Babyn Yar ravine. During the years of the Nazi occupation, there were also close to 100,000 other victims buried there: Gypsies, Russians, and members of other nationalities, as well as many prisoners of war of various ethnic groups, including Ukrainians.

• *In my city of Stryi, where there was an almost equal number of Ukrainians, Poles, and Jews; the ethnic balance was markedly changed by the ethnic cleansing carried out by both the communists and the Nazis. By 1959, the Jewish population was drastically reduced to just very few, while a new group took over and stayed for decades: the Russians. Since so many Ukrainians were either sent to Siberia, executed, relocated, or emigrated, Russians were brought in from Russia again to replace the decimated ethnic Ukrainian population. Thus, in the 1950s, Russians represented 30% of the population of Stryi.*

• *Many Ukrainians risked their lives to help Jews during the Holocaust, but to date there is no official record of the total number of Jews that they saved. Neither do we know the number of non-Jews, who risked their lives while attempting to save Jews, or, who were arrested or killed for doing this. Nor is there any documentation on the number of Ukrainian and Polish victims (or of victims from other ethnic or national groups), who were misidentified as being Jewish (as I was misidentified), and were executed.*

• *My generalization is based primarily on what I know about my and my family's friends. Those who took upon themselves to save Jewish or Christian individuals do not talk about it much, nor do many of those who were saved (some would refuse to admit publicly who saved them).*

Below, are examples primarily of Ukrainian and other individuals whom I know, who risked their lives to save their neighbors or complete strangers.

• *A Ukrainian family, the Abr.'s, hid and saved four Jewish friends and neighbors; only two of the survivors, who came to the USA after the war, admitted who saved them during the Holocaust. (Related to me by my friend, R. Abr.)*

• *My friend, R., accompanied a Jewish American family on a trip to a Ukrainian village in the early 1990s. This family wished to give several thousand dollars (a princely sum during that time!) to a poor Ukrainian farmer who had saved their parents during the Nazi occupation. The old man would not accept the money. He was rather embarrassed for being offered such a sum for helping a fellow human being and did not wish anyone to think that he had done this for the sake of a reward. These Americans made a mistake: they should have offered him a small token of appreciation rather than such a large sum that made him uncomfortable. When I visited my grandparents' graves in the early 1990s and met the man whose parents provided shelter to my grandparents, I, too, wished to give him some money. He would not accept it, but was very grateful for small American souvenirs.*

• *(Even individuals helping large numbers of Jews and non-Jews, who were persecuted, did not talk about it much. Neither did the British financier, Nicholas Winton, who, at the beginning of WWII, saved 669 Jewish and other Czech children from Czechoslovakia and brought them to Britain as part of the Kindertransport project. It was only in 1988 that his wife accidentally found lists of the children's names, and realized the scope of his mission. It was then that the world learned of his humanitarian action.)*

• *In New Jersey, where we lived for 48 years, I had two very good Jewish friends, who owed their lives (or their parents did) to the Christians who saved them. One of them is F. Before she was even born, a Ukrainian family was able to save her parents. F. had never met members of that Ukrainian family, yet continued to write letters to them and, in gratitude, kept sending token gifts even to the third generation of her parents' saviors. F.'s husband even learned Ukrainian in order to correspond with them. However, another friend, L., felt only disgust towards her savior because of the rude attitude and terrible surroundings where a poor Polish woman had to hide my friend, who was then 7 years old. Even though, in this case, the woman was well compensated, she still had to risk her own and her family's life for undertaking this.*

• *Among the Jews who were saved by various members of my family, and/or our close friends, was a leading Rabbi Aharon Rokeach (1880-1957) of Belz. My son-in-law's mother (and also*

my friend since 1948), Maria Shkilnyk Leshchyshyn, described to
me the period during the Nazi occupation, when she was about 15
years old, while her father, Dr. Mykhailo Shkilnyk (1891-1972), was
mayor of a Western Ukrainian town, Peremyshliany. He was an
attorney, who had earlier served in the Ukrainian National Rada
(headed the Consular Section), and later was a practicing lawyer
and judge, as well as community leader, in Peremyshliany, for over
20 years. People often turned to him in times of need. During the
German occupation, at the end of July 1941, Nazis began organized
attacks on Jews. The town Jewish delegation approached Mr.
Shkilnyk with a request to shelter the Great Rabbi Rokeach, who
fled to Peremyshliany that year. Mr. Shkilnyk agreed, even though
it meant risking the lives of his wife and three children. After
considering various hiding places, he decided to turn a deserted
three-storied house into a storage facility for electrical equipment,
and put up a sign to that effect on the front door. He then directed
a trusty electrician (A. Zilber) to manage it and "find" a live-in
"watchman," who was to be the Rabbi. The Shkilnyk family, who
lived three houses down the street, shared with the Rabbi whatever
food was available.

The Rabbi was sheltered there until August 1942, when a
Hungarian colonel with several officers, all wearing Hungarian
uniforms, came by car to see Mr. Shkilnyk at his home, asking about
the Rabbi. The colonel then went to see the Rabbi, bringing him
gifts of food and money from the Jewish community in Hungary.
Following this, the Rabbi sent word, asking Mr. Shkilnyk to see him.
During the visit, the Rabbi informed him that with the gifts from
Hungary, there is no need to share the family food supplies with him.
He proudly treated Mr. Shkilnyk to dried fruit and Tokay Hungarian
wine. Several weeks later, somehow Gestapo officers learned about
the Rabbi and took him away. In the fall off 1943, the Rabbi's sister
(or cousin) came to see Mr. Shkilnyk, with the news that the Rabbi
was taken to Bochnia, a town near Krakow.

After the war, Mr. Shkilnyk learned that Rabbi Rokeach
was fortunate to have reached Israel via Hungary. In 1948, the
Shkilnyk family settled in Winnipeg, Canada. Rabbi Rokeach
managed to get the Shkilnyks' address, and sent them a letter from
Israel, expressing his gratitude for risking their lives in sheltering
him in Peremyshliany, during the Nazi occupation. He also sent
his blessings to each member of the Shkilnyk family.

Whenever Dr. and Mrs. Shkilnyk talked at home about "the Hungarian colonel," that visited them, they called him Raoul Wallenberg, the way he introduced himself in their house.

The author interviewed Maria Shkilnyk Leshchyshyn several times, between 24 and 30 September, 2016. Dr. Shkilnyk left his family a 6-page typed description of the sheltering of Rabbi Rokeach in Peremyshliany. An abridged text of this was published as "Rescue of the Great Rabbi", in: Yakov Suslensky, "They Were True Heroes", Kyiv: Society "Ukraine", 1995, 64-68. ISBN5-7707-67778-2.

• *In a recently published interview, a Holocaust survivor describes his Ukrainian saviors.*

Roald (Safran) Hoffman, born in Zolochiv in 1937, during the Nazi occupation, was sheltered by a Ukrainian family, Mykola and Maria Diuk, in Univ, near Zolochiv. Mr. Diuk, a teacher, hid the young Roald, the latter's mother, two uncles, and an aunt for 18 months. Roald Safran Hoffman later became a chemist and professor at Cornell University; in 1981, he received the Noble Prize in chemistry. He relates that while hiding from the Nazis, he was able to observe several Jewish boys who were sheltered by Ukrainian Greek Catholic monks at a near-by monastery in Univ; among those boys was a Polish diplomat and the future Minister of Foreign Affairs of Poland (in 2005), Adam Daniel Rotfeld.
http://www.forumdaily.com/amerikanskij-nobelevskij-laureat-spasyonnyj-ukraincami/ (Read on 9.23.2016, 9:51am)

• *If you know any WWII survivors, or their families, ask them how they managed to get through all the tough times of the war. Ask them if there was anyone who offered them a helping hand or even risked their lives in order to shelter them?*

• *If you know any descendants of survivors of the Ukrainian famine – the Holodomor (1932-1933) – ask them how their ancestors survived, and if there was anyone who helped them?*

Notes to Chapter 6

MARIA, WHO WOULDN'T BE SAVED

• *The Nazis forcibly took 3-5 million young people from Ukraine, Belorussia, and Russia to work in German factories and farms and called these slave laborers "Ostarbeiter" [workers from the east]. Among them were children as young as 12 years old. In 1942 alone, Hitler brought to Germany half a million Ukrainian girls over 15 years of age.*

• *The Nazis also kidnapped some 10 to 20 thousand Polish and Ukrainian children, who had physical attributes similar to those of Germans (blond and blue-eyed). They were then assigned to German families to be brought up as Germans. This was part of the German "Lebensborn Program" (introduced in 1935), meant to balance a declining German birthrate and ensure continuity to the German race. Marsha Forchuk Skrypuch, in her biographical book "Stolen Child" (Toronto: Scholastic, 2010), describes the fate of a Ukrainian girl who was kidnapped and raised as a German.*

To prevent similar crimes, the UN passed the following definition of genocide (Article 2, the Convention on the Prevention and Punishment of the Crime of Genocide, 1948): "any of the following acts committed with intent to destroy, in whole or in part, a national, ethnical, racial or religious group, as such: killing members of the group; causing serious bodily or mental harm to members of the group; deliberately inflicting on the group conditions of life calculated to bring about its physical destruction in whole or in part; imposing measures intended to prevent births within the group; [and] forcibly transferring children of the group to another group." http://www.un.org/en/preventgenocide/adviser/pdf/osapg_analysis_framework.pdf (Read on 30 November 2014, 4:59 pm)

• *The night before their retreat (late June 1941) from Ukraine, when the Nazi forces were advancing, Soviet forces massacred political prisoners. Religious leaders tried to prevent any possible demonstrations of revenge on those who were known to have collaborated with the communists. However, when the Nazis arrived, they used the situation to inflame interethnic distrust, and blamed Jews for collaborating with the Soviets.*

• *The Ukrainian Greco-Catholic Archbishop Andrei Sheptytsky wrote letters of protest December 1941 and February 1942) to Henrich Himmler (in charge of the Nazi protection squadron) against the policy of annihilation of Jews in Western Ukraine. On 29-31 August 1942, he also wrote to Pope Pius XII, calling such Nazi actions, bordering "on an insane national-chauvinism."* https://uk.wikipedia.org/wiki/Андрей_(Шептицький). *(Read on 14 August 2016, 13:14.)*

• *To prevent people from submitting to the Nazi instigation of reprisals against communist Soviet collaborators and their suspected role in the massacres, the Archbishop sent out a letter to the faithful on 21 November 1942, summoning them to help the persecuted Jews. He also threatened to excommunicate from the Church those, who would instigate or participate in any killing of Jews. He called upon all faithful Ukrainian Greco-Catholics to shelter Jews.*

• *Ukrainian priests alone saved 183 Jews; among them was Dr. Leon Chameides, who was sheltered by Archbishop Andrei Sheptytsky. Dr. Chameides had his memoir published (in 2012) under the title "Strangers in Many Lands: The Story of a Jewish Family in Turbulent Times." He was the son of a prominent rabbi in Lviv, and in 1942 was saved (at the age of 7), together with his brother (age 9) by the Archbishop. Similarly, the teenage son of the Chief Rabbi, Ezekiel Lewin, was sheltered by Archbishop Sheptytsky, first in Lviv, and later in a monastery in the town of Univ.*

• *There are also numerous examples of Ukrainian priests and their faithful, who risked their own lives to save fellow human beings. Rev. Omelian Kovch (of Peremyshliany), father of six children, was arrested by the Nazis for refusing to stop sheltering hundreds of Jews, and in 1944 was executed in the Majdanek concentration camp.*
(Rev. Dr. Borys Gudziak, "The Witness of the Ukrainian Catholic Priest-Martyr of Majdanek, Omelian Kovch", The Ukrainian Weekly, September 2, 2012, p.7.)

• *The Ischchuks, parents of my former professor at the University of Pennsylvania, lived in the Ukrainian city of Rivne; they sheltered several Jewish families and individuals from actions by the Nazis. By doing it, the Ischchuks endangered not just the adults in their own family, but also their two teenage daughters. Since the family had many Jewish friends whom they wished to help, they would either provide shelter for them or find a way for them to escape to a safe place. Among the Jews that the Ishchuks helped in 1943, in Rivne, were: Mr. Perlman, a merchant; the Gudz family; Dr. Schuchman, a dentist and his family; and the Rosenberg family. One of the women sheltered by the Ishchuks, was caught and admitted where she was hiding and who helped her. Only by chance, did the Ishchuks manage to survive. In 1991, Rider College (later Rider University) Holocaust and Genocide Center, in Lawrenceville, N.J., honored one of their daughters, Prof. Natalia Ishchuk Pazuniak for her family's efforts in saving Jewish families.*

(See: Rider College, Occasional Paper Series, no. 7. Interfaith Remembrance Service Honoring Raoul Wallenberg and Roman Ishchuk. Lawrenceville, N.J. October 1991.)

• *Mr. O.Z., my Ukrainian friend in Ellicott City, MD, told me in 2014, that he was rereading his diary from the 1940s, written when he was still in his teens. He was always interested in books but did not have money to buy them. When he went to high school in the town of Sniatyn, he used to spend time browsing in the only bookstore in town with Ukrainian books. Then, he learned that the owner of the bookstore was held in the Jewish ghetto, where food was very scarce, so O.Z. decided to help the bookstore owner and his family. At night, he would crawl under a wire fence, and deliver food. His Jewish acquaintance, in turn, wished to reciprocate somehow, and gave him old Ukrainian history books, particularly, several by Mykhailo Hrushevsky, the leading Ukrainian historian. The young man could not have afforded to buy these unique books (published over two decades previously). O.Z. told me that the reciprocated gift not only contributed to his own education, but also influenced his intellectual interests and life choices; although he became an engineer, he also started a publishing house of historical books dealing with Ukraine.*

Notes to Chapter 7

AND WHERE IS MY BROTHER?

• *It was in the late 1950's, that by means of rather cryptic indirect correspondence of our friends, my family found out the shattering news about my brother's death in 1955. There were thousands of other families that have been similarly split by WWII, and never learned what happened to their loved ones who had joined the insurgents / freedom fighters in the Ukrainian Partisan Army (UPA), an anti-Nazi and anti-Soviet resistance movement, or who were sent to the Siberian GULAGs.*

• *In the fall of 2014, I talked to Daria M., whose family was very helpful to us during our wanderings across Western Europe, in the last months of WWII. Daria was with her parents and one of her brothers, Lubomyr. She also had another brother, Zenon (Zenko) who stayed behind, in Ukraine. He was a very principled and outspoken person in reference to any injustices. The family lived in Zolochiv, in the western part of Ukraine. One day, in 1944, during the Nazi Occupation, while he was at the local railroad station, he witnessed a train arrive, pulling freight cars full of 15-25 years old men and women. He immediately grasped what was happening: Nazis were taking these young people, either as slave laborers (Ostarbeiter), or to concentration camps in Germany. He ran to the back of the train and unlocked the doors of several cars. This enabled many of the young people to slip out quietly. Since the German guards were watching the cars only from the front of the station, it took them a while to learn that the cars were emptying.*

Although the young Ukrainians quickly left the cars and the area, someone noticed that it was Zenon who let them out. Leaving the station, he ran home to notify his parents what happened at there, and that he was joining the Ukrainian freedom fighters. Thousands of young Ukrainians were joining the insurgency movement in order to fight against the Nazis, as well as the Soviets. These young people felt a personal and patriotic obligation to stand up against both invaders. Also, it seemed to be the last chance in the twentieth century to try to regain independence for Ukraine. Many of them continued that fight in the UPA until the mid-1950s, and some even in later.

By the end of the day, the Gestapo was knocking on his parents' doors but did not find Zenon at home. During the night, the family packed quickly and left. Sadly, they never heard from him again, and never received any news of him. They never found out whether the Nazis or the Russians were responsible for the presumed death of their son and brother.

(Daria M., Zenon's sister, interviewed by the author, on October 15, 2014.)

• *There were occasions when Ukrainian insurgents were successful in their attempt to stop the Nazis from taking large numbers of young people to perform hard labor or to be sent to concentration camps in Germany. Each year on July 16, Ukrainians in the town of Z'horany (Volyn region), commemorate the 1943 battle against the Nazis, when the Ukrainian insurgents managed to stop and rescue a train full of young people being transported to Germany. (www.Day.ua, July 31, 2014. Read on 31 July 2014, 15:58).*

Notes to Chapter 9

WHY ARE ALL THE REGIMES AFRAID OF YOUNG SCOUTS?

• *In Part I, I mention Rev. Artemiy Tsehelsky, our gentle parish priest in Stryi. At that time, little did we all know, that in 1946, not even a year after the Soviets occupied western Ukraine again, they not only suppressed, but also outlawed the Ukrainian Greco-Catholic Church. However, Rev. Tsehelsky refused to change his faith to the Russian Orthodox; for this, he was arrested and sentenced to 7 years of hard labor in Siberia. When we later heard about it, I wondered how this affected his hands, and especially his fingers, since he was an excellent violinist. After he served his time, he was not allowed to resume his work as a Greco-Catholic priest, and earned his living as a teacher of violin and musical theory.*

Addendum to Chapter 10

JUST A TEMPORARY FAREWELL TO UKRAINE?

• *In the nineteenth century, in Central and Eastern Europe, there was a Slavophile movement, claiming that all Slavic nations had the same, or similar origins and were much like brothers. In 1928, the Czech artist Alphons Mucha (1860-1939) created a series of 20 large canvasses "History of Czechs and Slavs." Based on this popular work, he is credited with resurrecting the earlier Slavophile movement. Many Czechs and Slovaks were brought up on such teachings; the emphasis on common Slavic roots was further strengthened by a negative reaction to the earlier German occupation.*

Notes to Chapter 11

TWO MORE EXECUTION ATTEMPTS

• *Slovaks proved to be very kind and trusting people. Since they hated Germans for occupying their land, at first they blindly trusted Russians, because they too were Slavs.*

• *The Soviet regime supported the use of the misnomer "Russian" for "Soviet." Outside of the USSR, Soviet communists and soldiers were generally known as "Russians," since Russian was the official language in all of the Soviet republics, which were tightly controlled by Moscow. In the USSR, besides the Russian Republic, there were 14 other Soviet Republics. Theoretically, all these republics were equal, but one of them was more equal than the sum of all the others.*

Notes to Chapter 16

FORCED "REPATRIATION" TO — SIBERIA?!

• *In reference to the Yalta agreements, the Ukrainian refugees felt lower than pawns. It was as if they were some Lilliputians with whose fates three giants were carelessly playing. Yes, the Allies giants! The One from the East knew what he wanted and insisted on it. The other two were so eager to appease and to please him that they gave up countries and territories that belonged to the Lilliputians. None of the giants even thought of asking the people from those lands what they wanted, needed, or deserved. Even borders were moved, leaving some refugees without a country, while many local people were dislocated accordingly.*

No wonder that after the war – a war of nerves began, while the stateless refugees felt misunderstood, misidentified, and misrepresented in the heart of their very own Europe!

• *George F. Kennan (who, in 1951, became the American ambassador to the USSR) claimed that "the world community would suffer" if the refugees refused to return. It did not matter what would happen to the refugees, as if they were not part of the "world community!" Western Allies simply did not wish "to offend the Soviets," as Arthur Koestler depicted this in his book Scum of the Earth (1941).*

• *After World War II, the eastern part of Europe was split into two parts. The easternmost part was ceded to the USSR, under Moscow's hammer and sickle. According to the new American concept of "containment" (introduced by the American diplomat George F. Kennan), the arrangement was intended to "contain" Russia's constant expansion into foreign countries. Nevertheless, there was also a general acquiescence for some countries to be buffer zones, or Soviet "satellites." Among the European satellites were Bulgaria, East Germany, Poland, Hungary, Romania, Yugoslavia, and Czechoslovakia. A cement wall, the so-called "Berlin Wall," was erected soon in that city, symbolizing not just a physical and political, but also a psychological divide of Berlin, of Germany, as well as the whole of Europe. Border crossings between the Soviet and communist countries and the West were tightly controlled. Even train rails between some satellite countries and the Soviet Republics had to be readjusted to a different track gauge (each time a train was to pass the border), so that no Soviet citizens could escape on a fast train. I observed this myself when travelling from Budapest (Hungary) to Chop (Ukraine), in 1988. It was an unbelievable and surrealist scene: The same gauge continues to be used in many post-Soviet countries.*

• *During WWII, the U.S., United Kingdom, and Russia / USSR were Allies against Hitler. At the Yalta Conference (February 1945), Stalin convinced Roosevelt and Churchill to have all former Soviet citizens repatriated, including people from the new lands that the Molotov Ribbentrop Pact handed over to the USSR (e.g. western Ukraine and the Baltics). Moscow even promised that the "former citizens" would be welcomed with open arms. However, few refugees who had previously experienced the Russian regime were willing to return to their home countries, which were now under Soviet occupation. "To return," most likely meant to be arrested, sent to the GULAGs of Siberia, or to be executed. To most refugees, returning to the Soviet Union was worse than death – and they communicated this to the American soldiers and officials.*

• *Allida M. Black, in her biography of Eleanor Roosevelt, describes discussions at the UN's Social, Humanitarian and Cultural Committee, to which E. Roosevelt had been assigned. The committee had to deal with the problem of WWII refugees, particularly the displaced refugees who were afraid to "return to their countries of origin because of their political views." Mrs. Roosevelt opposed such forced repatriation, and was able to achieve passage of the Universal Declaration of Human Rights in 1948, which stated that "everyone has the right to seek asylum from persecution." She continued her mission, until 1951. "Each time the Soviet recommendations were voted down by sizeable margins and ultimately the UN and its subsidiary agency, the International Refugee Organization, came down in favor of resettlement rather than repatriation."* https://www2. gwu.edu/erpapers/abouteleanor/erbiography.cfm *(accessed on 9.21.2014, 15:20).*

Notes to Chapter 17

IN SEARCH OF SAFETY IN GROUPS: THE AUGSBURG CAMP

• *The meeting, in 1945, with the poet Lesia Ukrayinka's eldest sister was my first direct contact with a member of the highly respected, prominent Ukrainian cultural leaders, the Kosach family. Many years later, in 1976, I met the poet's youngest sister, Isydora Kosach Borysova. I was then a lecturer at Rutgers University (after writing my doctoral dissertation, which included a chapter on Lesia Ukrayinka's "In the Wildnerness," a drama about Pilgrims in Massachusetts and Rhode Island). Together with Ms. Kosach Borysova, I had the honor of unveiling the statue of Lesia Ukrayinka in Kerhonkson, New York.*

• *For more information on post-WWII Ukrainian DP camps, see: V. Kubijovyč, Ukraine. A Concise Encyclopaedia* (Toronto: U. of Toronto, 1963), I. 912.

• *Russia's habit of invading Ukraine continues into the twenty-first century: in 2014 Russia occupied and annexed Crimea (as it did in 1793), and still in 2016 continues to maintain a partisan war in the eastern part of Ukraine. After annexing Crimea, the Russian government immediately acted against the Ukrainian*

Greco-Catholic Church there, by confiscating its holdings, including the church building. Ukrainian language books, held at various Crimean institutions, including universities, were burned on February 2015. The Russian government in Crimea banned both the Ukrainian Greco-Catholic Church and even the Ukrainian Orthodox Church of the Kyiv Patriarchate (which is not under the jurisdiction of the Moscow Patriarchate). Russia is also restricting Crimean Tatar indigenous groups from keeping their traditional social structures and cultural activities. All Tatar movements are controlled and their leaders are often detained and / or arrested.

Notes to Chapter 19

A BREATH OF NORMALCY FOR THE YOUNG IN CAMPS

• *The post-war Displaced Persons (DP) camp schools and high schools (Gymnasia) were accredited by the German Department of Education and were registered with UNRRA. All the Ukrainian DP schools belonged to a coordinating office, with an inspector who would visit the schools. In this manner all Ukrainian DP schools managed to keep similar course programs, and use the same textbooks.*

• *Ivan Bahrianyi (1907-1963) was a Ukrainian poet, playwright, and a popular novelist. His bestselling novel "Tyhrolovy" (1944) was published in an English translation as "The Hunters and the Hunted" (London, 1956).*

• *See summary of a lecture by Prof. Orest Subtelny at the Ukrainian Museum in New York City, 7th March 2003, http://www.ukrainianmuseum.org/news_030311subtelny-DPcamps.html (Read on 21 February 2015, 16:25)*

• *Roman Voronka, personal correspondence to this author, 14 February 2014.*

• *George Orwell's book "Animal Farm" (both the original, as well as all translations) was banned in the USSR until 1989. The title of the first (1947) translation into Ukrainian was "Kolhosp Tvaryn," [literally: "The Animal Collective Farm."] There are now at least three newer translations into Ukrainian, published in the U.S. and in Ukraine.*

Notes to Chapter 20

UNEXPECTED ENCOUNTERS AND KIND DEEDS

• *Just as I was finishing my first draft of these reminiscences, I read Iryna and Marko Mostovych's story of their father's life at the end of WWII. Leonid Mostovych, a medical student, and his brother Mykola, both young idealistic Ukrainian nationalists, were arrested by the Nazis, and held for two years in several Nazi concentration camps. Later, I learned that Leonid Mostovych was held at first in Auschwitz, then Mauthausen, and finally at Melk (a subcamp of Mauthausen, situated north of Linz). While sick and on the verge of starvation, he was forced to walk for miles to this camp. When he had no strength left to dig tunnels in granite rock, he passed out from hunger. He was thrown on a heap of dead bodies to be burned alive the following morning. That was on the 5th of May, when Americans liberated the camp. While detecting some signs of life in Mostovych, an American soldier started shaking him to stop him from losing consciousness, offered him a saltine cracker (the only food item he had in his pockets), and then carried him in his arms to a military first-aid center. This saved Leonid Mostovych's life. He completed his medical studies and came to the United States, where over the course of more than 30 years, he concentrated on providing professional help to American veterans. He specialized in the medical problems of veterans, taught at the Medical School of the University of Kentucky, and headed the Radiology Department at the Veterans Medical Center. He considered it his duty to repay to all American veterans the kindness that was extended to him in 1945, by a soldier whose name he never learned. When Dr. Mostovych retired, he kept asking his wife whether he had actually succeeded in repaying his debt to that American soldier.*

Sources: Iryna Mostovych-Deychakivska and Marko Mostovych ("Podzvin po nashomu bat'kovi," Svoboda, June 8, 2012, p.19). Also, a phone interview with Dr. Mostovych's widow, Oksana Mostovych, on June 27, 2016. She is the author of a book of sketches "Zahublenyi Samotsvit"([A Lost Gem], Kharkiv, 1999), including one depicting how an American soldier saved her husband's life.

Chapter 24

ADDENDA

A. UKRAINIAN HISTORICAL TIMELINE

B. MY MATERNAL FAMILY ODYSSEY TIMELINE

C. GLOSSARY

D. ACKNOWLEDGEMENTS

E. INDEX OF NAMES

A. UKRAINIAN HISTORICAL TIMELINE

HISTORICAL EVENTS in UKRAINE
which influenced the lives of my ancestors and my family

9ᵗʰ-13ᵗʰ Century: the state of Kyivan Rus (pronounced "Roos") includes most of today's Ukraine, plus additional territories to the North and North East (Belarus and parts the future Muscovy).

988 /987-989/: the Kyivan Rus state, headed by its grand princes, officially accepts Christianity from Byzantium.

1187: first recorded usage of the name "Ukraine" in historical chronicles.

1595: religious leaders discuss union between western leaning Christian churches (Catholic) and eastern (Orthodox) ones.

1596: At the Union of Brest, many Ukrainian (Ruthenian) bishops (including the Metropolitan of Kyiv) sign a treaty with the Vatican, acknowledging that their Ukrainian Greco-Catholics, as an Eastern Catholic Church, would be "in communion with the pope." Bishops of Lviv and Peremyshl join later.

1648-1711: Ukrainian Kozaks defend the land from the neighboring Poland, Muscovy, and Turkey.

1654: Treaty of Pereiaslav, a pact of cooperation between Ukraine and Muscovy (later renamed as Russia). However, despite the treaty, Muscovy annexes Ukraine to its realm.

1686: Moscow Orthodox Patriarchate takes over the Kyiv Orthodox Metropolis.

1709: Battle of Poltava: Ivan Mazepa, Hetman of Ukraine, attempts to throw off Moscow's domination by inviting Sweden's help. The alliance loses the war against the Russian tsar Peter I.

1713: Peter I changes the name of the kingdom of Muscovy to "Russia" (basing it on the original name of the Kyivan Rus state), and in 1721 calls it Russian Empire.

1793: After the Second Partition of Poland, Russia claims Ukrainian lands up to the Zbruch River.
April 8: Empress Catherine II gives Ukrainian Greco-Catholics in the Russian Empire only 24 hours to accept Russian Orthodoxy or lose priestly rights and nobility privileges.
Russia annexes Crimea.

1793-1939: Zbruch River serves as part of the border between the Russian and the Austrian, and later the Austro-Hungarian Empires; Poland administers and controls parts of the western territories of Ukraine.

1863: Russian Empire bans Ukrainian publications, claiming that "there is no Ukrainian language, and never can be."

1913-1914: WWI

1914-1915: Russia invades and occupies Western Ukraine.
Russia arrests the head of the Ukrainian Greco-Catholic Church, Archbishop Andrei Sheptytsky, along with many priests, cultural, and political leaders.

1917: Ukraine proclaims it's own state.

1918: Ukraine proclaims independence.
March 3: Brest-Litovsk Peace Treaty between Soviet Russia and the Central Powers (Austria-Hungary, Germany, Poland and Bulgaria, and the Ottoman Empire) ends Russia's participation in WWI. Russia recognizes Ukraine's independence, while Poland is to administer western Ukrainian territories.
Nov 1: Western Ukrainian National Republic proclaims its independence from the Austro-Hungarian Empire and Poland. Western Ukraine invites all national minorities (Poles, Jews et al.) to send their representatives.

1919, *Jan. 18:* Paris Peace Conference favors "the preservation of the territorial integrity of the Russian Empire" and "sanctions the Polish occupation of Galicia."
Jan 22: Unification Day of Ukrainian lands; Western Ukrainian National Republic joins the Ukrainian National Republic.

1920, *April 22:* with the Treaty of Warsaw, Ukraine cedes Western Ukrainian territories to Poland.

1921: Peace Treaty of Riga (between Poland, the Russian SFSR, and the Ukrainian SSR): armistice is achieved, establishing borders between Poland and USSR. The border remains valid until 1939.

1932-33: Soviet government organized famine, called the *Holodomor* (death by starvation), which takes the lives of 4.5-7 million Ukrainian farmers/peasants, unwilling to join collective farms.

1930s: Moscow continues persecuting Ukrainians: a. intellectual elites (academics, writers, political, cultural, and religious leaders); b. peasants/farmers (leading to huge human losses of life during the *Holodomor*); c. language (periodic Party dictates change rules governing the Ukrainian language, in order to bring it closer to the Russian). Together, these aspects represent an actual genocide of Ukrainians carried out by the Soviet regime.

1939, *Aug. 23:* The Molotov Ribbentrop Pact (or Stalin-Hitler Treaty of Non-Aggression between Germany and the USSR) is signed in Moscow. It divides Eastern Europe into occupations between the two partners, with western parts of Ukraine assigned to the Soviet Union (together with the eastern part of Ukraine, the Ukrainian Soviet Socialist Republic).
Sept. 1: Nazi Germany invades Poland.
Sept. 17: USSR takes over Belarus and western parts of Ukraine.

1941, *June 22:* German/Nazi Army pushes the Soviets out and occupies Western Ukraine.
June 21-29: as the Soviets retreat, they massacre Ukrainian and Polish prisoners (mostly political prisoners) in many cities.
The Nazis inspire inter-ethnic reprisals directed at individuals and groups that collaborated with the Soviets.

1945, *Feb.6-11:* Yalta Conference (held at Yalta, Crimea) between Franklin D. Roosevelt (USA), Winston Churchill (United Kingdom), and Joseph Stalin (USSR), discussing such postwar issues as: the surrender of Germany; the reorganization

of the Polish government and delineation of new borders; Soviet annexation of western Ukraine; compulsory repatriation of all Soviet citizens. USSR is to take from Japan the Kurile Islands (all except the two just north of Japan).
June 26: the Ukrainian Soviet Socialist Republic becomes one of the 51 founding members of the United Nations.

May 8, End of World War II
1946, *March 1:* The Soviet regime arrests Ukrainian Greco-Catholic Church leaders, bans the Church, and forces the faithful to join the Russian Orthodox Church.

1954: Russian Soviet Socialist Federated Republic transfers Crimea to the Ukrainian SSR.

1990, *Jan. 21:* Demonstrating national unity, and honoring the Ukrainian independence proclaimed in Kyiv in 1919, 3 million people hold hands, forming a long symbolic Live Chain across the territory of Ukraine.

1991, *Aug. 24:* Ukraine proclaims its independence from the Soviet Union.
Dec 1: National Referendum on the independence of Ukraine is supported by 92% of the population. Leonid Kravchuk is elected President.

1994, *Dec. 5:* The Budapest Memorandum provides security assurances by the USA, United Kingdom, and Russia, relating to Ukraine's sovereignty and territorial integrity, once Ukraine hands over its nuclear warheads (i.e. accession to the Treaty of Non-Proliferation of Nuclear Weapons).

2013: Russia inspires and leads a war to break away the Donbas region (in eastern Ukraine) from Ukraine.

2014, *March:* Russia attacks the Ukrainian peninsula of Crimea, occupies it and annexes it by force (holding mock elections, even allowing the occupying Russian soldiers to vote).
A lengthy popular protest of Ukrainians (at the *Maidan*) against President Yanukovych, forces him out of office.
May: Petro Poroshenko is elected President.

B. MY FAMILY ODYSSEY TIMELINE

1793–1939
• The Zbruch River serves as part of the border between the Austro-Hungarian and the Russian (later Soviet) Empires, splitting Ukraine into two parts
• in 1793 my ancestor, Toma Shankovsky, and his two brothers, flee from the new rule of the Russian Empire to the Austro-Hungarian Empire, rather than submit to Catherine II's decree to renounce within 24 hours his Greco-Catholic religion and identity

1914
• Russia invades Western Ukraine
• Mother's brother, Mykola Shankovsky, killed in battle, while defending Ukraine from the Russian invasion

1939
• Aug. 23: the Molotov Ribbentrop Pact (or Treaty of Non-Aggression) between Germany and the Union of Soviet Socialist Republics (USSR), splits Eastern Europe into two spheres of influence: that of Nazi Germany and the Soviet Union
• Sept 1: Germany occupies Poland and western Ukraine

WORLD WAR II BEGINS
1941
• June 22: Germany invades the Ukrainian part of Galicia
Shocking views of massacred political prisoners by the retreating Soviet forces.
• June 23-24: Germany invades Soviet Union (incl. the Ukrainian Soviet Socialist Republic)

1944
• July 24: our family leaves Stryi in a truck, and later on a train, going *west*
• We cross the border to Poland and then Slovakia
• Sept. 1: together with a train full of Ukrainian refugees (in freight cars), we arrive in Slovakia: Banska Bystrica and then Krupina
• Sept. 7: we are stationed in Nemce
• Sept. 12: change of flags in town: first, a Slovak one, then a communist (Soviet partisan) Red flag

- Sept.14: Soviet partisans cross the border to Slovakia
- Oct. 22: German tanks and cars appear
- Oct. 30: our group of 33 Ukrainian refugees boards a freight car again
- Nov. 1: on a train to Bratislava, weface visible threats of execution by Soviet partisans, who then postpone the event until the following morning
At night, a daring Slovak train engineer dares to save us by rushing the train away from the area
- Nov. 2: the Strasshof Internment Camp (Austria); Vienna
- Nov. 7: train to Dresden
- Nov. 8: Leipzig
- Nov. 9: Possen
- Nov. 15: Magdeburg; stay in a camp
- Nov. 21: Potsdam; Frankfurt
- Nov. 22: Frankfurt; Possen
- Dec. 1: Wroclaw to Vienna
- Dec. 3: Vienna to Gattendorf
- Dec. 11: Gattendorf to the Vienna suburb, of Semmering
- Dec. 12: Vienna: in search of our friend, Dr. Skoretska
- Dec. 13: Wienerneustadt
- Dec. 4: the ski-town of Semmering

1945
- Feb. 6: Vienna
- Feb. 7: Jedlorsdorf
- Feb. 8: Gmintz, Jeger
- Feb.11: Pössneck (Thuringia)
- April 8: Pössneck bombed and RR tracks damaged
- Apri 14: spend the night in a bunker
- April 15: American troops arrive; white flags appear on houses in Pössneck
- April 25: Polish police arrive
- May 4: unidentified airplanes above; canon shooting nearby
- May 7: Germany surrenders
- May 8: official German surrender

END OF WORLD WAR II

- May 9: Russian soldiers threaten to "repatriate" Ukrainian refugees to the Soviet Union

- May 15: Father goes to Kahl, trying to confer/help 3,000 Ukrainian refugees in the camp, who are purposefully misidentified as "Russian"
- May 18-19: Russians arrive with an American army support, but under red flags
- May 20: Ukrainians ordered to leave Pössneck and register with Russian Repatriation representatives; refugees protest
- June 1: many Soviet cars arrive under their own flag
- June 6: Soviets demand that their zone include Saxony and Thuringia
- June 10 (?): leave Pössneck, since it is in Thuringia, which is to become part of the Soviet Zone
- July-August: long and slow road to Augsburg, in the American Zone
- Sept. 3: register at the Sommerkaserne Ukrainian DP camp in Augsburg
- October: transfer to Reinhardt-Kaserne Ukrainian DP camp in Neu-Ulm

1948
- April 15: report to Funk-Kaserne, in Munich, to begin our emigration processing to Canada
- May 3: receive Canadian visa and continue numerous screenings
- Sept.17: depart from Europe to Canada, on Cunard's S.S. Samaria
- Sept. 28: arrive in Quebec City, Canada.

C. GLOSSARY

(Words marked by *, have a separate entry in this Glossary)

Allies/Allied Powers. During World War II (1939-1945), the following countries were known as Allies: United States, Great Britain, France, and the Soviet Union.

Animal Farm. The British writer, George Orwell's 1945 satire of Soviet falsehoods and tyranny.

Aryan. Hitler claimed that the German people and their race ("Aryan" or Nordic) were superior to others.

Axis Powers. A coalition of countries opposing the Allies*: Germany and Italy, later also Japan. The Axis signed the Tripartite Pact, on 27 September 1940.

Babunia or Babusia. Grandmother, in Ukrainian

Babyn Yar (in Ukrainian; in Russian – Babiy Yar). Name of a ravine on the outskirts of Kyiv, where the Nazis executed more than 200,000 people. On 29 September 1941, the first massacre was of Jews (33,761 victims). Nazis tried to justify this act as a response to sabotage by Soviet agents (see: Serhii Plokhy, *The Gates of Europe. A History of Ukraine*, 2016, p. 270). Later, people of other nationalities were also executed. Present estimate of victims: about 50,000-60,000 thousand Jews, 40,000 Ukrainians, and close to 100,000 total of Russians, Gypsies, Soviet prisoners of war (from all nationalities), communist activists (of various nationalities), and other unknown victims. A leading Ukrainian poet, Olena Teliha* (head of the Union of Ukrainian Writers) and her staff of the literary journal *Litavry*, were executed at Babyn Yar on 22 February 1942. The Nazis particularly persecuted the Organization of Ukrainian Nationalists: 621 of its members were executed there between 1941-1943.

Berlin Wall. After WWII, the Wall inside the city of Berlin represented part of a borderline between the communist East

Germany and the free West Berlin. The Wall stood there from 1961 to 1989, to keep people from defecting to the West. It was a symbol of a political and psychological barrier between the communist countries of Central and Eastern Europe, and the rest of Europe and the Free World. The Wall served as part of the "Iron Curtain*," since it psychologically kept people of the communist countries from crossing to the West. Close to 5,000 East Germans managed to escape to the West through the Wall, while about 138 died in unsuccessful attempts.

Brest Litovsk Peace Treaty. The Treaty was signed on 3 March 1918, between the Ukrainian National Republic and Germany, Austro-Hungary, Turkey (the Ottoman Empire), and Bulgaria. As a result, Russia recognized the independence of Ukraine. However, the treaty also determined Ukraine's borders; western and northwestern Ukrainian regions (parts of Volyn, the Kholm/Chelm area, and Pidlashshia) were ceded to Poland, while Galicia and Bukovyna were to remain part of Austro-Hungary. The Treaty was terminated in November 1918.

Calendar, Old. Many Eastern or Byzantine, Greco-Catholic, and Orthodox Christians celebrate Christmas according to the "Old" or Julian calendar, which, in this century, is 13 days later than the "New" or Gregorian calendar. The difference of 13 days represents a correction between the two calendars. Thus, for example, Christmas according to the "Old" calendar, is still celebrated on December 25, on the Julian calendar; but that day falls on the "New calendar" on January 7th.)

Catafalque. An elevated platform (similar to a table) on which a coffin with a dead body is placed for funeral services.

Catholics. There are two major branches of the Catholic Church: the Roman Catholic and the Eastern or Greco/Greek Catholic*; both of them recognize the Pope. Greco-Catholic priests are allowed to marry prior to their ordination.

Convention on the Prevention and Punishment of the Crime of Genocide. Adopted by the United Nations General Assembly on 9 December 1948 (as General Assembly Resolution 260).

Containment. A term coined in 1945 by George F. Kennan of the US Department of State, during WWII. It applied to policies attempting to "contain" Russia's constant western expansion. However, it also enabled Moscow to control the bordering countries in the west and south of Europe, keeping them under communism as "satellites:" Albania, Bulgaria, Poland, Romania, East Germany, Hungary, Czechoslovakia, and Yugoslavia.

Crimea (Krym, in Ukrainian). Ukrainian peninsula on the Black Sea. Occupied and forcefully annexed by Russia in 2014. From the tenth through eleventh century, for over 200 years, Crimea was part of the Kyivan Rus kingdom. Then, there were periods when it was controlled by the Mongols, Venetians and Genoese, Crimean Tatars and the Ottoman Empire. In the seventeenth century, the population was composed of 95% Crimean Tatars, 3% Greeks, and 2% Armenians. In 1783, Russia annexed and held it for 171 years. In 1853-56, during the Crimean War, France, Britain, Sardinia, and the Ottoman Empire fought against Russia, who claimed to be protecting the 13% of Russians who resided there. Russia ruled over Crimea until it was annexed by the Soviet Union in 1920. In 1944 Russia ousted all Tatars, Armenians, Bulgarians, Greeks and other minorities from the Crimea, leaving only Russians (75%) and Ukrainians (21%). After this ethnic cleansing, Khrushchev gifted Crimea to Ukraine in 1954. Since the renewal of the independence of Ukraine, Crimea remained an integral part of the Ukrainian state.

Didunio, dido, didus. Grandfather, in Ukrainian.

DP, Displaced Persons. The DP's were refugees, the largest group among them, were Ostarbeiter*, forcibly taken by the Nazis* from their countries during WWII. The other refugees included former political prisoners, POW's, and those who voluntarily fled their lands when communists invaded East-European countries. At the end of WWII, there were over16 million refugees in Germany; among them about 2.3 million Ukrainians. The Allies*, with the support of international aid organizations (UNRRA* and IRO*), provided refugees with temporary shelter in camps, in Western Germany and Austria (1945-1949), until their resettlement elsewhere. When the

Soviets demanded that the Allies immediately repatriate the DPs, many refugees refused to return, however when threatened that harm would come to their families, the refugees complied; others were taken by force with the acquiescence of the Allies. Of those repatriated, many thousands were executed, and tens of thousands were sent to labor camps in the Far East. About 200,000 Ukrainian refugees refused to "return home," and over 150 thousand remained in camps for 2-3 years, until their resettlement to North and South America and other western countries. Only about 22,000 Ukrainians remained in West Germany. (See Orest Subtelny, *Ukraine. A History*, 1988, p. 557.)

Encolpion cross. A cross (approx. 5 inches long) that opens up on a hinge (at the top), like a box. It has a hollowed inside, holding pieces of a saint's relics, or the True Cross of Christ.

Exorta. Introductory remarks or discussion (which could be held in another room or building), prior to the reading of the Gospel in church.

Fellow Travellers. Popular name for sympathizers or supporters (not members) of the Communist Party.

Galicia (Halychyna). The westernmost region of Ukraine. Since the end of the tenth century, it was part of the Kyivan Rus state. At the turn of the thirteenth century, Galicia/Halych joined Volyn, another principality of Ukraine, and in 1272 the city of Lviv became the capital of this united state. In 1340, Poland attacked Galicia and Volyn, and ruled over them until 1848, when both became part of the Austro-Hungarian Empire. In 1914, Russia invaded Galicia and occupied it until the middle of 1915. In 1918, Galicia proclaimed its independence as a Western Ukrainian National Republic. On 22 January 1919, this republic joined the central Ukrainian National Republic, thus uniting most Ukrainian ethnographic territories. In 1921, Galicia reverted to Poland. A 1923 document specified that the administration of this territory is to have a degree of autonomy for Ukrainians. Soviets occupied Galicia from 1939-1941; Nazi Germany occupied Galicia 1941-1945; and, Soviets again, 1945-1991, until Ukraine regained its independence.

Genocide. Raphael Lemkin, the author of the term "genocide," defined it as follows: "Genocide is directed against the national group as an entity, and the actions involved are directed against individuals, not in their individual capacity, but as members of the national group." The United Nations General Assembly officially recognized the term on 11 December 1946, specifying that the term genocide refers "to the physical aspects, as well as to cultural and linguistic aspects of the crime." In 1953, in speech in New York Lemkin, stated that the Ukrainian famine, called *Holodomor**** (artificially created by the Soviet government), was a *Ukrainian genocide*, since it included the destruction of cultural, religious, ethnic, and demographic aspects of Ukraine.

Gestapo. Secret State Police of Nazi* Germany; also active in Nazi-occupied countries during WWII. Considered to be cruel and heartless robots in carrying out their plans, especially in reference to all the non-German "Untermenschen*."

Gothic script. A German script of the Latin alphabet used in Germany from the Middle Ages until 1946. There were several variants of the script, with typically rather pointed lettering.

Greco-Catholics, Ukrainian Greek Catholics, or Ukrainian Catholics.* Ukrainian Catholics of the Eastern branch of the Catholic Church. Occasionally called "Uniates", since they joined/united with the Catholic Church.

GULAGS. Soviet Union's Main Administration of Corrective Labor Camp System, from 1918 until 1988. The term is often used for various places of exile for persons sentenced to forced labor. There were 53 such camps and 423 labor colonies in the coldest parts of the Soviet Union, such as Siberia. At different times, there were from 2 to 17 million inmates, 20% of them Ukrainians.

Gymnasium. A European middle and high school system with eight grades (following four grades of primary school). Such schools were either classics oriented (with obligatory Greek and Latin courses), or with concentration in math and sciences.

Halychyna. The south-western region of Ukraine. This is the Ukrainian term for the central-eastern European Galicia;* the majority of its population is Ukrainian.

Holocaust. Hitler's Nazi Germany planned to annihilate people of "the lower races": first Jews and Gypsies, then the Slavic nationalities. Holocaust refers to the 6 million Jews who were killed between 1939-1945. It is the third monstrous European genocide (preceded by the Armenian massacre and the Ukrainian Holodomor*) of the twentieth century.

Hitler, Adolf (1889-1945). Leader of Germany's National Socialist-Democratic Party (Nazi Party); creator of the Nazi* ideology of German superiority and the need to expand the German living space by means of conquest of peoples and territories. As dictator of the Nazi regime, he was responsible for the killing of millions of non-Germans, particularly, Jews, Gypsies, as well as Slavic nationalities.

Holodomor. Literal meaning "death by hunger." A Kremlin directed genocide that starved to death 4.5 to 7 million of Ukrainian farmers/peasants in 1932-33. (See *Genocide**.) Grain was confiscated from the farmers and exported. Millions of Russians were later brought in to settle in the empty Ukrainian villages and to work in heavy industry in the area.

Herr. Mister (in German).

Hrushevsky Mykhailo (1866-1934). In 1917-1918, served as the head of the Ukrainian Parliament, the Ukrainian Central Rada. He was a statesman, leading scholar, and dean of Ukrainian historians, as well as cultural and political activist, and a dominant public figure. He also headed the Shevchenko Scientific Society, that acted as a Ukrainian academy of sciences.

I.R.O. International Relief Organization aiding WWII refugees in Western Europe.

Iron Curtain. The term was coined by Winston Churchill on 5 March, 1946. It "formed the imaginary boundary dividing

Europe into two separate areas from the end of World War II in 1945 until the end of the Cold War in 1991. The term symbolized efforts by the Soviet Union to block itself and its satellite states from open contact with the West and non-Soviet-controlled areas." (En.wikipedia.org/wiki/Iron_Curtain." Read on 21 October 2016)

Judenrat (Jewish Council, in German). The Nazi regime required Jewish ghettos (in Central and Eastern Europe) to have their own council to administer the daily life of Jews in there. The Judenräte had their own *police force*, in charge of ensuring that all Jews had moved to ghettos; some also had to pick who was to be sent to hard labor or death camps.

KGB. "Committee for State Security of the Soviet Union" (in Russian; 1954-1991), performing both internal policing and foreign intelligence. A highly feared institution with great powers over human lives in all the Soviet Republics. Formerly known as the NKVD.

Kozaks. Ukrainian volunteer military groups/formations, active in central Ukrainian regions from 1475 to 1775, defending the land from foreign invasions. Their primary base was the Zaporizhian Sich (an island on the Dnipro River).

Kurile (Kuril) Islands. A series of islands (56 total), just north of Japan. Most of them (39) were claimed by Japan in the seventeenth century. In the eighteenth century, Russia began to claim them. In 1855 a Treaty of Commerce, Navigation and Delimitation determined that all islands south of Iturup were to belong to Japan, and all those north of Urup to Russia; the Sakhalin Island was open to settlers from both countries. At the 1945 conference in Yalta (just prior to the end of WWII), President Roosevelt supported Russian/Soviet claims to the islands, except for the two southernmost large ones, that were to be left to Japan. Of the 56 islands that Russia governs now, only 9 are inhabited. 13% of the population, on the islands held by Russia, are ethnic Ukrainians; on the Etorofu/Iturup Island, the Ukrainian population exceeds 60%. The Ukrainian immigrants on the Kurile Islands are primarily former Soviet political prisoners (or their descendants), who had completed their sentences but were not allowed by the Soviets to return to Ukraine.

Lebensborn Program. Thousands of Polish and Ukrainian children, with physical attributes similar to those of Germans (blond and blue-eyed), were kidnapped and brought up as Germans, in German families.

Lebensraum [living space] – a German idea since the end of the nineteenth century that the country needed to colonize neighboring lands to provide more living space and food in order to survive. Hitler developed the concept further (1921-25), focusing on Eastern Europe and Ukraine, in particular. This provided an excuse for Germany's participation in WWII.

Lilliputians. Extremely small residents of an imaginary country "Lilliput," in Jonathan Swift's satire *Gulliver's Travels* (1726).

"My kingdom for..." Reference to Shakespeare's drama "Richard III", where the king exclaims: "my kingdom for a horse."

Molotov-Ribbentrop Non-Aggression Pact of 1939. Also known as the Ribbentrop-Molotov, or Stalin-Hitler Pact. Stalin and Hitler divided among themselves most of Eastern Europe. The central and eastern Ukrainian territory was to be ruled by Russia/USSR, and the western-most (western Ukraine) by Poland. Within weeks, Germany invaded Poland, and the Soviets took most of the western Ukrainian lands.

Napevno. In Ukrainian: assuredly, indeed, for certain. Opposite to *nepevno*.*

Name Day. Popular in Ukraine and many parts of Europe, celebrating the day of the saint, in whose honor a person was named.

Nazi, Nazis. Shortened form for Germany's National Socialist-Democratic Party (the Nazi Party, 1931-1945), headed by Adolf Hitler*. This mass party had its own specific Nazi ideology of German superiority, much of it expressed in Hitler's autobiography *Mein Kampf*. Since 1933-1945 only the Nazi Party was allowed in Germany and Austria.

Nepevno: uncertain, not certain.

NKVD. A powerful andthreatening Soviet secret police, precursor of KGB.*

Ostarbeiter. Worker from the East (Ost), slave laborer brought by force by the Nazis from Eastern Europe to Germany during WWII.

Patria. Latin for own country, or homeland.

Pershyi Vinok [The First Garland] published in 1887; 2nd ed. 1984. An anthology of poetry, prose, and essays written and published by Ukrainian women writers.

Plast. Ukrainian Scouting*. Established in 1911. Banned by all foreign occupiers of Ukraine (Soviet since 1920; Polish in 1930, Nazi 1941). After WWII, Ukrainian refugees continued their scouting activities in many countries of the free world. Ukrainian Plast Scouting was re-established in Ukraine in 1990.

Potsdam Conference (17 July–2August 1945). Held by the United Kingdom, France, USA, and USSR in the town of Potsdam, Germany. The text of their Agreement was presented on 2 August 1945. It described how the Allies were to divide Germany into "zones" administered by each of the four Allied partners. The Soviet Union was given the eastern part of Germany, which became "East Germany" (German Democratic Republic), while the other three zones (occupied by Great Britain, France and the USA) were combined into "West Germany," or the Federal Republic of Germany. The city of Berlin was split between the two Germanies.

Resistance. Organized forces acting against an occupying power. During WWII, Ukrainian resistance groups (see UPA*) fought against the Soviets/Russians as well as the Germans/Nazis. Besides UPA, there were also small independent groups of partisans pursuing the same purpose.

Russian occupation of Western Ukraine. Czarist Russian forces occupied western Ukraine for several months in 1914-1915. Also called "first Russian occupation" in the twentieth century. It was followed by a Soviet occupation in 1939, and then in 1945.(Central and Eastern Ukraine were occupied by Soviet forces 1920-1941, and then 1945-1991.)

Ruthenians. Derived from the name "Rus" (Kyivan Rus) via Latin. From the eighteen century to 1900, it was applied to Ukrainians within the Habsburg Empire.

Scouting, Ukrainian Plast*. Established in 1911 on the same principles as the original British Scouting. Banned in Ukraine by all successive foreign rulers (Soviet in 1920; Polish in 1930, and Nazi in 1942). After WWII, Ukrainian refugees brought the movement to many countries in the West, where they had resettled. Plast-Scouting was re-established in Ukraine in 1990.

Sheptytsky, Andrey (1865-1944). Ukrainian Greco-Catholic archbishop (1901-1944) and prominent religious, cultural, and philanthropic leader. Member of the Austrian House of Lords (Parliament). He served as head of all Eastern Catholics in the Russian Empire. Arrested by Russians during their occupation of Galicia in 1914, he was held until 1917. He supported the self-determination of nations after the fall of Austro-Hungarian Empire and the Russian Empire. During the Nazi occupation, he wrote a letter of protest to the German representative in Galicia, criticizing the repression of Jews. Personally, he sheltered many Jews and Ukrainians who were persecuted by the Nazis.

Shevchenko, Taras (1814-1861). The greatest Ukrainian poet and artist, a revered bard and a poet-prophet figure. His works continue to be widely read by all levels of society.

Siberia. Russian-held areas in the east and north of Asia (stretching all the way to the Pacific Ocean). Since the seventeenth century, used by the Russian Empire to send political opponents, as well as criminals, for punishment and exile; since the nineteenth century, prisoners were being sentenced to do hard labor. The system continued to be used by the Soviet Union. Millions of Ukrainian, Polish, and Russian dissidents (among them many leading writers), as well as other nonconformists, and people from all walks of life, were exiled to Siberia, where many died due to harsh weather conditions, as well as hard labor and malnutrition.

Slavs, Slavic nationalities. The following nationalities are Slavic: Belarusians, Bosnians, Bulgarians, Croats, Czechs, Macedonians, Montenegrins, Poles, Russians, Serbians, Slovaks, Slovenians (or Slovenes), Ukrainians, and others. They occupy central, south-eastern and eastern parts of Europe.

Soviet occupations of Ukraine. From 1920-1941, Soviets occupied eastern and central areas of Ukraine; also Western Ukrainian* areas 1939-1941. Most of Ukraine became part of the Ukrainian SSR from 1945-1991.

Soviet Union. USSR (Union of Soviet Socialist Republics) 1922-1991. It was a conglomerate of nations under the strict dictatorship of Moscow, with only token national rights for the 14 non-Russian republics. Even although the Soviet constitution allowed individual republics to leave the union, none of them dared to try this until 1991.

Stalin, Joseph (1878-1953). Communist dictator of the USSR (1929-1953), ruled over all the Soviet Republics with cruelty, organizing purges, and genocide of millions (e.g. the Ukrainian artificial famine, the Holodomor). He held his position by creating extreme fear, terror, suspecting all, and causing denouncements even by family members. The Communist Party was the only party allowed in the USSR, and it acted on Stalin's orders and wishes.

Stryi. A western Ukrainian town, now in the Lviv region (oblast), southwest of the city of Lviv, near the foothills of the Carpathian Mountains. Located on the banks of the Stryi River.

Svitovyd statue. A ninth century, four-sided statue, facing four sides of the world. Found in the Zbruch River (Galicia, Ukraine) in 1848. Since 1851, the statue is at a museum in Krakow, Poland.

Teliha, Olena (1907-1942). Poet and literary critic. Headed the Ukrainian Writers Union, and served as editor of its publication Litavry. Together with her husband and the editorial board of the periodical, was arrested in Kyiv by the Nazis, and executed in Babyn Yar on 22 February 1942.

211

The True Cross. The cross, which is believed to be the one on which Jesus Christ was crucified.

Ukayinka, Lesia (Larysa Kosach Kvitka, 1871-1913). Leading Ukrainian poet, playwright, and a strong supporter of human rights for all. She is primarily cherished for her verse drama, stressing an individual's choice of principles. She is one of the earliest European existentialist playwrights.

UNRRA. United Nations Relief and Rehabilitation Administration, created in 1943 to help WWII refugees in Western Europe.

USSR. Union of 15 Soviet Socialist Republics (including the Ukrainian Soviet Socialist Republic).

Übermenschen. Literally, "supermen." Nazis* claimed that they were of an "Aryan" or Germanic race, biologically superior to others. Based on some ideas by the German philosopher, Friedrich Nietzsche.

Ukrainian Catholics, or Greco-Catholics*, or Ukrainian Greek-Catholics*. Ukrainian Catholics are members of the Eastern branch of the Catholic Church.

Untermenschen. Nazis considered all non-Germanic people to be of a subhuman or inferior race.

UPA. Ukrainian Partisan Army (1942-1950's), an armed Resistance formation of insurgents fighting against the Nazis and the Soviets during and even after WWII.

VSUM (Ukrainian Youth Educational Society). In 1942, representatives of the underground Ukrainian Plast Scouting organized VSUM. By circumventing Nazi laws that did not allow Scouting, this organization provided an opportunity for youngsters to attend summer camps.

World War II (WWII: 1939-1945). During WWII, Ukraine lost about a fifth of its population: 5 million were ethnic Ukrainians, and about 2 million from other ethnic groups, including about a million of Jewish victims of the Holocaust.

Yalta Conference, 4-11 February 1945. Meeting between Roosevelt, Churchill and Stalin at the Ukrainian city of Yalta, in the Crimea. They agreed on several actions to be taken at the end of WWII, such as: assigning most of Western Ukraine to the USSR, and repatriating all the refugees from the former Soviet territories to the Soviet Union, as well as from new ones, such as Western Ukraine.

Zbruch River. It served as part of a political border; from 1793 to 1939 between the Russian Empire and the Austro-Hungarian, and, since 1939-1941, between the Soviet and Polish ruled western Ukrainian territories.

D. ACKNOWLEDGMENTS

It is a most inspiring experience when one can call upon friends and colleagues during a writing process. I am deeply grateful for the unfailing moral support and/or assistance that they provided to me before this book became a reality. These individuals had either shared with me some scenes about my family's past, or simply fulfilled the role of my moral and informational virtual support staff.

The virtual presence also refers primarily to old letters, documents, or even photographs from centuries past. They were immeasurably inspirational during the writing about my war experiences, in particular those, which were influenced by earlier historical events. As a teacher, my mother, Maria Shankovska Zaleska, was always interested in history and read widely on European and church history. She often related various stories about her family, and compiled a genealogy of her father's line, the Shankovskys. Not having access at the time to any documents in Ukraine (as long as it was still part of the USSR), my mother often discussed family history with her distant cousin, Lev Shankovsky, who was a historian. Both of them were WWII refugees, who came to North America with just a few pieces of luggage and very few documents. In the 1970s and 1980s, they corresponded incessantly with each other, trying to piece together their common lineage.

In 2011, when my husband and I moved from New Jersey to Columbia, MD, our parish priest, the Very Reverend Taras Lonchyna, organized a series of presentations about Ukrainian Catholic priests in the parishioners' families. It was initially for this purpose that I started putting on paper a few of the stories related by my mother about my Shankovsky grandparents and their line of priests. I started locating them on the basic genealogical tree that my mother made. Later, my cousin Martha Shankovsky Shmorhun, and I, while doing more research on our family, were able to fill in many lacunae; Martha also constructed a detailed genealogical tree of our branch of the Shankovsky line.

It was then that one of my grandsons, Danylo, started asking me about my family's experiences during WWII. That moment served as another strong catalyst to start assembling my reminiscences about my family's past. There were so many stories that I soon started recounting them occasionally to my family and friends. Then, about five years ago, when sorting my parents' documents, I found a treasure trove: my father's, Tadey Zalesky's, mini journals. He would note only a word, a phrase, a sentence, or just the name of the city where we were on a given day during WWII. If he had a spare moment, he would write even several sentences.

I also rediscovered my own diaries that I started writing in 1945. Together, these treasures offered a reasonable framework and reference sources to start putting on paper my own recollections about the war. By that time, my parents were long gone. However, on both sides of my family, I am fortunate in having several cousins, who read my first drafts, and corrected or added some information about our family. On my paternal side, Lida Zaleska Stasiuk and Christina Zaleska Shepelavey were particularly helpful in this respect. On my maternal side, Dusia Balatska Kovalchuk. Christine Nehrebetsky, and Martha Shankovsky Shmorhun shared with me many old family photographs. I was fortunate to be able to discuss the post-war Displaced Persons camp period with friends from my Gymnasium years, Tania Prushynska Tkachenko, Roman Voronka, and Yaroslav Fedun.

The shaping of the text took several years, as well as a multitude of drafts. I am grateful to several of my colleagues, who served as a sounding board and critics of my early text. I am much indebted to Columbia Writers Guild (who met regularly at Columbia's Oakland Manor); my gratitude is addressed especially to Phyllis Geiger, Lynada Johnson, and Pat Engelbach, for their patience in listening to and commenting on parts of my numerous drafts. I am very grateful to Cher Madden and Lada Onyshkevych, who helped me with copy-editing and/or proofing various parts of the manuscript. My friend Elehie Natalka Skoczylas not only provided me with sound advice in reference to specific details in the text, but she also stepped in by inputting editing changes in my text, when problems with my shoulder prevented me from doing it myself. Myroslava Znayenko helped decipher many documents written in several languages. Vasyl Lopukh was my patient technical advisor, especially in terms of layout assistance, and my son Boyan Onyshkevych decoded some mysteries in my technical problems. My husband Lubomyr Onyshkevych served as my captive audience, sounding board, and monitor of historical data.

My good friend Mykhailo Komarnytsky, of Litopys Publishing in Lviv, took charge of preparing a camera-ready copy with the help of Andriy Vasyliv. I am most grateful to the artist, Ann Ladyk, who sensed the tone of my reminiscences and found an elegant way to depict it on the cover. My thanks goes also to all my five grandchildren, who were 11 through 17 years old when I started writing my text in 2014: Lukash, Ruslan, and Roman Onyshkevych, as well as Danylo and Sophia Leshchyshyn. They dutifully read my complete second draft (willingly, I hope!), shared many comments, and gave the text more than a passing grade. It is they who particularly pressed me to publish it.

While so many were most helpful, I may not have always taken their good advice, and as a result made my own errors. I apologize for the latter.

LARISSA M. L. ZALESKA ONYSHKEVYCH

Acknowledgement of Permissions to Reprint

I would like to express my gratitude to the following editors and publishers who granted their kind permissions to reprint maps, photographs, and/or artwork:

Ms Taisiia Haidukevych, editor of *Stryi* (2007), for reproduction of photographs of the Stryi prison and its logbook (1941), and an artistic rendering of the Stryi prison and victims (oil, 1941) by Petro Savchyn. Reprinted with permission of the editor.

The Drohobyczer Zeitung (Drohobych, Ukraine), Oleh Stetsiuk, editor, for permission to reprint a photograph of Nazi and Soviet soldiers at a friendly meeting in September 1939, near Drohobych http://www.drohobyczer-zeitung.com/2012/10/drohobych-during-period-of-nazism-foto.html. Reprinted with permission of the editor.

Ukrainian Internet Encyclopedia (Dr. Marko Stech, Director) *Map of Ukrainians in Displaced Persons Camps in West Germany and Austria, 1946-1950*. Drawn by Dr. Ihor Stebelsky. Reprinted with permission of the director/publisher.

University of Toronto Press
Map 23 (Western Ukraine during the interwar period, p. 426) and Map 25 (Ukraine under German rule 1941-44, p. 468, from *Ukraine: A History*, 1ˢᵗ edition, by Orest Subtelny, ©University of Toronto Press, 1988. Toronto, Buffalo, London. Reprinted with permission of the publisher.

The map "Ukrainian Soviet Socialist Republic, 1939" (p. 441) from *Encyclopedia of Ukraine*, volume 5, edited by Danylo Husar Struk, ©University of Toronto Press Incorporated 1993. Toronto, Buffalo, London. Reprinted with permission of the publisher.

Vsevolod A. S. Z. Onyshkevych: graciously provided photographs of the Svitovyd statue.

E. INDEX OF NAMES
*(NB: all clergy marked "Rev." here are priests of the
Ukrainian Greco-Catholic Church)*